RECIPROCAL TEACHING at Work

Strategies for Improving Reading Comprehension

Lori D. Oczkus

Orinda, California, USA

INTERNATIONAL
Reading Association
800 BARKSDALE ROAD, PO BOX 8139
NEWARK, DE 19714-8139, USA
www.reading.org

Director of Publications   Joan M. Irwin
Editorial Director, Books and Special Projects   Matthew W. Baker
Managing Editor   Shannon Benner
Permissions Editor   Janet S. Parrack
Acquisitions and Communications Coordinator   Corinne M. Mooney
Associate Editor, Books and Special Projects   Sara J. Murphy
Assistant Editor   Charlene M. Nichols
Administrative Assistant   Michele Jester
Senior Editorial Assistant   Tyanna L. Collins
Production Department Manager   Iona Muscella
Supervisor, Electronic Publishing   Anette Schütz
Senior Electronic Publishing Specialist   Cheryl J. Strum
Electronic Publishing Specialist   R. Lynn Harrison
Proofreader   Elizabeth C. Hunt

Project Editor   Sara J. Murphy

Cover Credits   Design: Linda Steere; Photographs (from top): PhotoDisc, Brand X, Image Productions

Copyright 2003 by the International Reading Association, Inc.

All rights reserved. No part of this publication may be reproduced or transmitted in any form or by any means, electronic or mechanical, including photocopy, or any information storage and retrieval system, without permission from the publisher.

Web addresses in this book were correct as of the publication date but may have become inactive or otherwise modified since that time. If you notice a deactivated or changed Web address, please e-mail books@reading.org with the words "Website Update" in the subject line. In your message, specify the Web link, the book title, and the page number on which the link appears.

Library of Congress Cataloging-in-Publication Data
Oczkus, Lori D.
  Reciprocal teaching at work : strategies for improving reading comprehension /
Lori D. Oczkus.
      p. cm.
Includes bibliographical references and index.
  ISBN 0-87207-514-1 (pbk.)
  1. Reading comprehension. 2. Reading (Elementary) 3. Cognitive learning. I. Title.
  LB1573.7.O39 2003
  372.47--dc22   2003016148

Eighth Printing, July 2006

For Bryan, Rachael, and Rebecca

CONTENTS

ACKNOWLEDGMENTS

Writing a book is an enormous undertaking that involves a great deal of stamina, motivation, and determination. I am convinced that the writing of this book would not have been possible without the support of many special people.

I am indebted to my knowledgeable band of teacher reviewers who carefully read every word of the manuscript and shared their honest suggestions, valuable insights, and constant encouragement: Audrey Fong, Joan Masaryk, and Ellen Osmundson.

Thanks are in order for the very talented group of researchers, educators, and authors who inspired my use of reciprocal teaching. I feel indebted to Annemarie S. Palincsar and the late Ann L. Brown for their groundbreaking research and the development of this successful teaching technique. Special thanks go to my longtime friends Dr. J. David Cooper, Irene Boschken, Janet McWilliams, and Lynne Pistochini for the development of an intervention with reciprocal teaching that has opened the doors to reading for many struggling readers. David also graciously read and responded to the manuscript.

Over the years, treasured friends have encouraged my teaching, staff development work, and now my writing. I'd like to extend special gratitude to MaryEllen Vogt, Susan Page, and Regie Routman.

I am grateful to Matt Baker, the International Reading Association's Editorial Director, for the invitation to write a book on this topic and for his writing expertise. Thanks also to Sara Murphy for her superb attention to detail and for keeping me on schedule.

Special thanks go to all the wonderful teachers who shared ideas, lessons, photos, and inspiration—Sandy Buscheck, Glorianna Chen, Lynne Hyssop, Susan Preble, Kristi Webster, Jill Hope, and Allison Krasnow—and the staffs at the following California schools: Randall in Milpitas, Hester in San Jose, Palmecia in Hayward, and Washington in Berkeley.

Judy Herns deserves recognition for pushing me to write this book! Thanks also to Linda Hoyt for her inspiration and encouragement to write for publication.

Thanks go to a group of very knowledgeable educators who cheered me on throughout the writing of this book: Nancy O'Connor, Pat and Bill Eastman, Gil and Mary García, Elaine Farge, and Alice Burkart.

Most of all, I appreciate my family for their unending support, love, and patience. The deepest of thanks to my husband, Mark, and our three precious readers, Bryan, Rachael, and Rebecca.

INTRODUCTION

The Reading Report Card for the Nation and the States (Donahue, Voekl, Campbell, & Mazzeo, 1999) reports that U.S. schoolchildren are lacking in basic reading comprehension skills. Students can decode words, but they have difficulty understanding what they read. As a staff developer and literacy coach, I have experienced this phenomenon firsthand: In the elementary schools where I work, which range from urban to suburban schools, many students have trouble summarizing or pulling main ideas from their reading. The students may complete a reading assignment and not even realize that they had problems understanding the text. Likewise, in my own bilingual, fifth-grade classroom, the students had difficulty reading and understanding the grade-level social studies text and literature anthology.

Teachers often complain that students cannot remember what they read and are not really engaged with the text. Recent reading research and my own classroom experiences emphasize that an urgent need exists for educators to teach reading comprehension strategies. Students at all grade levels need strategies for clarifying unknown words and ideas that they encounter while they read. Many students need modeling and guided instruction in answering and asking comprehension questions. What proven strategies can teachers use to improve their students' reading comprehension?

Reciprocal teaching is a scaffolded discussion technique that is built on four strategies that good readers use to comprehend text: predicting, questioning, clarifying, and summarizing (Palincsar & Brown, 1984). Although reciprocal teaching was introduced in reading journals in the 1980s, this research-proven technique for teaching multiple comprehension strategies is now becoming more widely recognized and used. The National Reading Panel (National Institute of Child Health and Human Development, 2000) advocates using cooperative or collaborative learning with multiple learning strategies and highly recommends reciprocal teaching as an effective teaching practice that improves students' reading comprehension. In cooperative learning with reciprocal teaching, students assist each other in applying the four reciprocal teaching strategies.

Originally, reciprocal teaching was designed as a paragraph-by-paragraph discussion technique in which the teacher would model each of the four strategies in a think-aloud, demonstrating the use of the strategies by talking through his or her thoughts while reading. Then, students would take turns "being the teacher" and using a think-aloud with each strategy. Since the original model was developed, however, the creators (Palincsar & Brown, 1984) and others (Cooper, Boschken, McWilliams, & Pistochini, 2000; Lubliner, 2001) have field-tested other models and teaching ideas that build on the original intent of reciprocal teaching. Regardless of the classroom setting, which may include teacher- or peer-led groups, the original goal of reciprocal teaching—to improve students' reading comprehension—is maintained. This teaching model allows the teacher and students to scaffold and construct meaning in a social setting by using modeling, think-alouds, and discussion.

The goals of reciprocal teaching are

- to improve student's reading comprehension using four comprehension strategies: predicting, questioning, clarifying, and summarizing;

- to scaffold the four strategies by modeling, guiding, and applying the strategies while reading;

- to guide students to become metacognitive and reflective in their strategy use;

- to help students monitor their reading comprehension using the four strategies;

- to use the social nature of learning to improve and scaffold reading comprehension;

- to strengthen instruction in a variety of classroom settings— whole-class sessions, guided reading groups, and literature circles; and

- to be part of the broader framework of comprehension strategies that comprises previewing, self-questioning, making connections, visualizing, knowing how words work, monitoring, summarizing, and evaluating (McLaughlin & Allen, 2002; Pearson, Roehler, Dole, & Duffy, 1992).

What the Research Says About Reciprocal Teaching

Palincsar and Brown (1986) found that when reciprocal teaching was used with a group of students for just 15–20 days, the students' reading on a comprehension assessment increased from 30% to 80%. According to a study by Palincsar and Klenk (1991), students not only improved their comprehension skills almost immediately, but they also maintained the improved comprehension skills when tested a year later. This powerful teaching technique is especially effective when incorporated as part of an intervention for struggling readers (Cooper et al., 2000) and when used with low-performing students in urban settings (Carter, 1997). Although originally designed for small-group instruction with struggling middle school students, reciprocal teaching has proved to yield positive and consistent results with primary- and upper grade elementary students who are taught in large-group, teacher-led settings and in peer groups (Cooper et al., 2000; Palincsar & Brown, 1984, 1986; Palincsar & Klenk, 1991, 1992). Rosenshine and Meister (1994) reviewed 16 studies of reciprocal teaching and concluded that reciprocal teaching is a technique that improves reading comprehension.

Lubliner (2001) points out that reciprocal teaching is an effective teaching technique that can improve on the kind of reading comprehension that is necessary not only for improved test scores but also for an information age. A growing need exists for students to learn sophisticated reading skills that they can employ in the workforce and in a world that is bursting with print materials and data. Students should be prepared to comprehend and evaluate a wide variety of complicated texts from books to electronic sources, and reciprocal teaching strategies can help them achieve that goal.

A Comprehensive Reading Comprehension Program

Even though reciprocal teaching is a powerful research-based teaching technique, it is not comprehensive enough to stand alone as a method for teaching reading comprehension. Reading is a complex process that has many facets, and reciprocal teaching was designed to focus on just four important strategies that good readers use to comprehend text. McLaughlin and Allen (2002) provide a broad framework for teaching comprehension that comprises the following eight strategies necessary for teaching students to understand what they read:

1. Previewing—activating prior knowledge, predicting, and setting a purpose

2. Self-questioning—generating questions to guide reading

3. Making connections—relating reading to self, text, and world

4. Visualizing—creating mental pictures

5. Knowing how words work—understanding words through strategic vocabulary development, including the use of graphophonic, syntactic, and semantic cueing systems

6. Monitoring—asking whether a text makes sense and clarifying by adapting strategic processes

7. Summarizing—synthesizing important ideas

8. Evaluating—making judgments

Some additional resources that will give you the big picture for teaching reading comprehension appear in Figure 1.

My Experiences With Reciprocal Teaching

When I speak to an audience of teachers and ask them if they have heard of or tried reciprocal teaching, depending on where I am in the United States, only a few hands go up. Sometimes, once I define the strategy, more heads nod with familiarity, but most teachers admit to having little experience with reciprocal teaching. I, too, had heard about reciprocal teaching and its effectiveness early in my teaching career, but in all my busyness, I placed this strategy on my to-do list and only dabbled in it a bit with my students. If I had known the incredible impact reciprocal teaching can have on reading comprehension, I certainly would have incorporated it into my teaching much sooner.

My interest in reciprocal teaching was awakened while I was serving as a literacy coach and consultant in an inner-city school in Berkeley, California, USA, where the staff and I used reciprocal teaching as part of an intervention for struggling readers (Cooper, Boschken, McWilliams, & Pistochini, 1999). Many of the intermediate students in our intervention read two or three years below grade level and, although they could decode words, were severely lacking in reading comprehension skills. After just three months of using the reciprocal teaching strategies with these students three times per week, we witnessed dramatic results. Many of the struggling students had jumped one or two grade levels in reading ability. We also saw their attitudes change from reluctant and negative to more confident and assured. We witnessed students who had struggled learn to love reading.

Figure 1
Resources on Teaching Reading Comprehension

Blachowicz, C., & Ogle, D. (2001). *Reading comprehension: Strategies for independent learners*. New York: Guilford.

Block, C.C., & Pressley, M. (2001). *Comprehension instruction: Research-based best practices*. New York: Guilford.

Cooper, J.D., & Kiger, N.D. (2001). *Literacy assessment: Helping teachers plan instruction*. Boston: Houghton Mifflin.

Duffy, G.G., & Roehler, L.R. (1987). Improving reading instruction through the use of responsive elaboration. *The Reading Teacher, 40*, 514–519.

Duffy, G.G., Roehler, L.R., & Herrmann, B.A. (1988). Modeling mental processes helps poor readers become strategic readers. *The Reading Teacher, 41*, 762–767.

Duffy, G.G., Roehler, L.R., Sivan, E., Rackliffe, G., Book, C., Meloth, M.S., et al. (1987). Effects of explaining the reasoning associated with using reading strategies. *Reading Research Quarterly, 22*, 347–368.

Duke, N.K., & Pearson, P.D. (2002). Effective practices for developing reading comprehension. In A.E. Farstrup & S.J. Samuels (Eds.), *What research has to say about reading instruction* (3rd ed., pp. 205–242). Newark, DE: International Reading Association.

Farstrup, A.E., & Samuels, S.J. (2002). *What research has to say about reading instruction* (3rd ed.). Newark, DE: International Reading Association.

Harvey, S., & Goudvis, A. (2000). *Strategies that work: Teaching comprehension to enhance understanding*. York, ME: Stenhouse.

Hoyt, L. (2002). *Make it real: Strategies for success with informational texts*. Portsmouth, NH: Heinemann.

Keene, E.O., & Zimmermann, S. (1997). *Mosaic of thought: Teaching comprehension in a reader's workshop*. Portsmouth, NH: Heinemann.

Kuncan, L., & Beck, I. (1997). Thinking aloud and reading comprehension research: Inquiry, instruction, and social interaction. *Review of Educational Research, 67*(3), 271–299.

Lipson, M.W. (2001). *A fresh look at comprehension*. Paper presented at the Reading/Language Arts Symposium, Chicago, IL.

McLaughlin, M. (2003). *Guided comprehension in the primary grades*. Newark, DE: International Reading Association.

McLaughlin, M., & Allen, M.B. (2002). *Guided comprehension: A teaching model for grades 3–8*. Newark, DE: International Reading Association.

McLaughlin, M., & Allen, M.B. (2002). *Guided comprehension in action: Lessons for grades 3–8*. Newark, DE: International Reading Association.

Miller, D. (2002). *Reading with meaning: Teaching comprehension in the primary grades*. York, ME: Stenhouse.

Pearson, P.D. (1985). Changing the face of reading comprehension instruction. *The Reading Teacher, 38*, 724–738.

Pressley, M. (2002). *Reading instruction that works: The case for balanced teaching* (2nd ed.). New York: Guilford.

Vogt, M.E., & McLaughlin, M. (Eds.). (2000). *Creativity and innovation in content area teaching*. Norwood, MA: Christopher-Gordon.

I asked myself, If reciprocal teaching yields such promising longitudinal results in an intervention group, why not weave this strategy into the fabric of classroom reading instruction so all students could benefit from it? So began my journey. As a literacy consultant and coach to many schools in the San Francisco Bay area and around the United States, I have shared reciprocal teaching with many teachers in myriad classrooms and at a variety of grade levels. As I continued using reciprocal teaching with struggling readers in various schools and settings, their teachers noticed that within a few weeks the below-grade-level readers became more confident and motivated readers. After more results revealed that the students had improved by one to two grade levels, I began to wonder if reciprocal teaching could be applied to other teaching contexts. I found research to support student growth in reading comprehension in a variety of settings, not just with struggling readers (e.g., Carter, 1997; Palincsar & Brown, 1984, 1986; Palincsar, Brown, & Campione, 1989; Palincsar & Klenk, 1991, 1992). Then, I began to experiment with reciprocal teaching in my regular classroom teaching during whole-class sessions, guided reading groups, and literature circles. Although it took time to introduce, model, and reinforce the reciprocal teaching strategies, the lessons were worth the effort as my students improved their use of reading comprehension strategies and their understanding. Because most of the students had some experience with predicting, questioning, clarifying, and summarizing, I built on their knowledge by presenting the four strategies as a package. My students enjoyed the engaging lessons and benefited from using reciprocal teaching throughout the day because we applied the strategies in content area reading.

I have used reciprocal teaching in every way possible to strengthen students' comprehension. I have taught reciprocal teaching strategies—predicting, questioning, clarifying, and summarizing—to the whole class by using Big Books and short newspaper and magazine articles. I have made reciprocal teaching bookmarks (see the Be the Teacher Bookmark on page 53 and the Clarifying Bookmarks on page 95) and used them to guide students as they applied the four strategies in guided reading groups. I have continued to give struggling readers an extra dose of reading comprehension instruction by using reciprocal teaching in special intervention groups (see Cooper et al., 1999). I have had students in literature circles take on the roles of the predictor, questioner, clarifier, and summarizer as they construct together the meaning of a text while deepening their understanding of the four strategies. I also have trained cross-age buddies in the second and fourth grades to focus on reciprocal teaching strategies as they read and discuss picture books together. By employing reciprocal teaching strategies in a variety of settings, we have provided students with many opportunities to use the strategies to improve their reading comprehension.

Why I Wrote This Book

This book will show you how to use reciprocal teaching in a variety of classroom settings to enhance students' reading comprehension. Although the results are consistently positive when teachers use reciprocal teaching, very little has been written about this teaching method. A search for reciprocal teaching resources primarily yields articles in reading research journals, although the model is mentioned in a few chapters in reading methods books, an intervention program (Cooper et al., 1999), and a teaching guidebook (Lubliner, 2001). Although all these resources are excellent and helpful, a need exists for additional classroom materials to support this highly successful reading comprehension strategy.

My goal in this book is to share many practical lessons to make reciprocal teaching accessible and enjoyable for teachers and students as they work together to improve the students' reading comprehension. The lessons in this book are geared toward grades 2–6; however, reciprocal teaching can be used successfully with K–8 students, so the lessons can be adapted for grade levels other than 2–6. In addition to lessons, I also want to share the various social contexts, or classroom settings, for using reciprocal teaching—whole-class sessions, guided reading groups, and literature circles. This book is designed to equip classroom teachers with this successful comprehension teaching technique so that, ultimately, it will enable teachers to improve their students' reading comprehension skills and attitudes toward reading.

Organization of This Book

I use reciprocal teaching in a variety of classroom settings to expand my teaching of it (see Figure 2), and my teaching method is slightly different in each setting. The chapters of this book are organized around the classroom settings and can be read in any order to suit the needs of your

Figure 2
Reciprocal Teaching in Different Classroom Settings

Classroom Setting	Why Use Reciprocal Teaching in This Setting?
Whole-Class Session	• to introduce the class to reciprocal teaching strategies • to establish common language and terms • to provide reinforcement in content area reading throughout the school day
Guided Reading Group	• to reinforce or introduce reciprocal teaching strategies in a teacher-led, small-group setting • to provide extra support or intervention to students who struggle
Literature Circle	• to release responsibility to students for reciprocal teaching strategies • to reinforce and strengthen student use of reciprocal teaching strategies

students and teaching style. However, I recommend reading chapter 1 first because it covers the rationale and important understandings central to reciprocal teaching, outlines the four reciprocal teaching strategies, and explains how to use them with students.

In chapter 1, each of the four strategies—predicting, questioning, clarifying, and summarizing—is described in detail, with ideas for prompting students to use the language unique to it. Because teachers sometimes encounter obstacles when implementing reciprocal teaching, the chapter includes practical ways to overcome such difficulties and information about the four critical foundations necessary for getting the most from reciprocal teaching: scaffolding, thinking aloud, thinking metacognitively, and learning cooperatively. The chapter also addresses common problems that students have with each strategy and provides suggestions for instructional support when these problems arise. Finally, suggestions for incorporating reciprocal teaching into a broader list of comprehension strategies are outlined to ensure a comprehensive reading comprehension program.

Chapter 2 offers lessons to introduce the whole class to the four reciprocal teaching strategies via depicting each strategy with a character, modeling the use of a variety of resources, and scaffolding with collaborative and partner activities. Bookmarks, posters, cooperative learning ideas, and lively minilessons assist students in remembering and internalizing reciprocal teaching strategies for eventual independent use.

Many ideas for leading students in reciprocal teaching discussions in guided reading groups are given in chapter 3. These teacher-led, small-group lessons can be the training ground for students' transfer to literature circles. The chapter includes a variety of suggestions for the use of graphic organizers, cooperative learning, fiction and nonfiction text strategies, and K-W-L lessons (Ogle, 1986) and ideas for teaching word analysis. In addition, intervention lesson ideas for struggling students are provided, along with suggestions for a creative intervention plan that involves moving the struggling students from reciprocal teaching in guided reading into leadership positions in literature circles.

Chapter 4 explores reciprocal teaching in literature circles, which is an excellent way to continue to provide students with opportunities to strengthen their use of reciprocal teaching strategies. Lessons for introducing the roles of predictor, questioner, clarifier, and summarizer are provided. The chapter also outlines a special discussion director position that rounds out the literature circle with prompts for connecting students' background knowledge and questions to the text. Many innovative tools such as role sheets, a discussion spinner, and minilessons on each of the four strategies are included. Finally, the chapter offers both students and teachers literature circle assessment tools.

The Conclusion summarizes the main points about reciprocal teaching as an effective method for teaching reading comprehension and offers a quick reference for readers who have a specific question about how or why reciprocal teaching should be part of their classroom agenda. In the chapter, teachers' common questions about reciprocal teaching are addressed in a practical question-answer format.

The appendixes comprise the following useful tools to support reciprocal teaching in the classroom:

- Appendix A: an assessment and observation rubric for predicting, questioning, clarifying, and summarizing
- Appendix B: a student self-assessment for the use of reciprocal teaching strategies
- Appendix C: feedback collected during informal assessment strategy interviews

Chapter Format

Chapters 2, 3, and 4 begin with a general overview format (see box), which is intended to describe and outline how reciprocal teaching enhances reading comprehension in that chapter's classroom setting.

Description of the Setting	• overview of what reciprocal teaching looks like in this setting
Goals	• goals of reciprocal teaching • goals of the particular setting
Organizing Your Classroom for...(whole-class sessions, guided reading groups, or literature circles)	• preparing for a particular setting, choosing groups when necessary, and selecting reading materials
The Big Picture (What Else to Do) in...(whole-class sessions, guided reading groups, or literature circles)	• realizing that reciprocal teaching does not stand alone • including other key comprehension strategies in this setting to ensure a comprehensive reading comprehension program • listing other key resources
Assessment Options	• overall suggestions for assessing reciprocal teaching and comprehension in the chapter setting

Following each chapter overview is a series of lessons that outline the procedures and rationale for scaffolding the lesson (see box on page 11 for lesson format). The lessons offer options for using reciprocal teaching to improve students' reading comprehension in the particular setting for that chapter, and two lessons in each chapter have accompanying classroom tales that show the respective lesson in action. (Student names in the classroom stories and elsewhere are pseudonyms.)

Reciprocal Teaching Strategies in This Lesson	• a list of the reciprocal teaching strategies addressed in the lesson
Background and Description	• thoughts and reflections on and experiences from using the lesson • brief description of the lesson • which reciprocal teaching strategies are emphasized and what else may be needed
Materials	• what supplies are needed for the lesson
Teacher Modeling	• providing scaffolded instruction; how to model the strategies for students
Student Participation	• releasing to students the responsibility for using the strategies
Assessment Tips	• assessing students using this particular lesson

Minilessons that focus on individual reciprocal teaching strategies are found near the end of each chapter and can be used when students need reinforcement for a particular strategy. The minilessons follow the same format and use the same headings as the longer lessons in each chapter. Keep in mind that reciprocal teaching strategies should be taught in concert with one another, so, if you focus on only one strategy during a minilesson, let your students know how that strategy fits back into the larger framework of all four reciprocal teaching strategies used to comprehend text. Remind your students that readers rarely use one strategy at a time while reading; instead, they use the four strategies together as they make their way through a text.

Each chapter ends with a list of key points for review and a series of reflections that can serve as a self- or group-study tool (see box on page 12).

Chapter Summary	• main ideas and vocabulary from the chapter • review of assessment tools
Reflections for Group Study, Self-Study, or Staff Development	• questions and discussion prompts to encourage conversations and reflections about the chapter material

This book extends the successful research of those who have so generously shared their reciprocal teaching ideas. The chapters are organized in a practical manner to make it easy for you to implement this instructional method in your own classroom. In addition to the many chapter features previously described, each chapter contains ready-to-use reproducible forms that will help students with understanding both the reciprocal teaching strategies and the texts that they are reading. The goal of this book is to provide you with the practical, motivating tools that you need to improve the reading comprehension of all students by using reciprocal teaching strategies.

CHAPTER 1

The Four
RECIPROCAL
TEACHING
Strategies

Predictions are based on facts from the book that lead you to what is likely to come next. Predicting gives you a feel for what you are reading and it makes you want to read more.

—Tanya, grade 6

Reciprocal teaching has four main strategies that teachers and students employ together to comprehend text: predicting, questioning, clarifying, and summarizing. I like to call the strategies the "Fabulous Four" or the "Be the Teacher" strategies because children can relate to and understand these terms. My students know that when I refer to the Fabulous Four I am directing their attention to a set of strategies that good readers use. They also know that the phrase "Be the Teacher" suggests that they take turns playing the teacher's role while using the strategies.

Each reciprocal teaching strategy has an important role in the reading comprehension process. The four strategies are part of a comprehensive reading comprehension program that is based on all the strategies that good readers use, such as previewing, self-questioning, visualizing, making connections, monitoring, knowing how words work, summarizing, and evaluating (McLaughlin & Allen, 2002). The order in which the reciprocal teaching strategies are used is not fixed; it depends on the text and the reader. For example, sometimes when I am reading a mystery with students, we naturally pause between chapters, bursting with predictions for what will happen next before we summarize, ask questions, and clarify the clues that we have so far. Other times, however, it may be more natural to summarize and clarify before making predictions and asking further questions.

This chapter offers a description of each reciprocal teaching strategy along with prompts to encourage students to use the language of a given strategy. The prompts provide students with the necessary support to become independent in the strategies, and, when combined with constant modeling of the strategies, they also help students to deepen their reading comprehension and ability to apply the reciprocal teaching strategies.

Predicting

Predicting involves previewing the text to anticipate what may happen next. Readers can use information from the text and their prior knowledge to make logical predictions before and during reading. When you are reading a piece of fiction with a class, lead the students through a discussion of the text structure of stories. Review elements usually found in fiction such as characters, setting, a problem, a resolution, and a theme or lesson. Prior to reading, have your students preview the book's covers, title, and illustrations to look for clues about the setting, characters, problems, and key events that may appear in the text. When reading nonfiction with a class, discuss the text's headings, illustrations, and other features, such as maps, captions, and tables, to allow your students to predict what they think they will learn from their reading. For either text type, stop periodically during the reading and ask students to gather clues and make predictions for the next portion of the text. In addition to discussing predictions, you can use a graphic organizer, such as a story map, that fits the text type. Giving students the opportunity to preview what they read by discussing text features and using graphic organizers provides them with visual clues for predicting.

The language that students may use with predicting includes the following phrases (Mowery, 1995):

> I think...
>
> I'll bet...
>
> I wonder if...
>
> I imagine...
>
> I suppose...
>
> I predict...

Predicting is a strategy that assists students in setting a purpose for reading and in monitoring their reading comprehension. It allows students to interact more with the text, which makes them more likely to become interested in the reading material while improving their understanding (Fielding, Anderson, & Pearson, 1990; Hansen, 1981). In my experience, students seem to enjoy predicting and do so with exuberance.

Questioning

Good readers ask questions throughout the reading process (Cooper, 1993; Palincsar & Brown, 1986), but formulating questions is a difficult and complex task. When students know prior to reading that they each need to think of a question about the text, they read with an awareness of the text's important ideas. They automatically increase their reading comprehension when they read the text, process the meaning, make inferences and connections to prior knowledge, and, finally, generate a question (Lubliner, 2001). During reciprocal teaching discussions, students can be asked to "be the teacher" as they create questions to ask one another that are based on important points in the reading.

I teach students to ask several types of questions during reciprocal teaching. However, we initially focus on questions that are answered in the text. Many students begin by asking questions about unimportant details. However, as I continue to model question formulation and students share their questions with the class, the quality and depth of their questions increase. Later in the process, I model how to ask questions based on inferences and main points in a text.

The language of questioning that students may use includes the question words *who, what, where, when, why, how,* and *what if.*

Most students who I work with enjoy asking questions or being the teacher during reciprocal teaching discussions. For example, during my weekly guided reading session with some second graders, I gave each student a self-stick note to mark the portion of text that he or she wanted to turn into a question. Billy became very enthusiastic every time he read silently with the purpose of generating questions. After marking a chosen page with his self-stick note, Billy would whisper to me at the reading table, "Mrs. Oczkus, I just found my question!" Students of all grade levels seem to have difficulty waiting to ask their questions, and they prefer to ask questions before they summarize, clarify, or predict the next portion of text. I have learned that it is best to take advantage of the students' enthusiasm, and I allow students to share questions with the group first. If we are short on class time, I will pair students and have them ask their partners questions, or I will have the students individually write down their questions.

Questioning is an important strategy for good readers. In reciprocal teaching lessons, students learn to generate questions about a text's main idea, important details, and about textual inferences, thereby improving their reading comprehension skills. In addition, questioning often becomes the favored strategy of many students.

Clarifying

Although students can be taught to identify difficult words readily and work through them, it is far more difficult for some students to recognize unclear sentences, passages, or chapters. Perhaps the difficulties occur because sometimes even though students can read every word in a given portion of text, they still do not understand the passage's main idea.

Clarifying helps students monitor their own comprehension as they identify problems that they are having in comprehending portions of text or figuring out difficult words. During this step of reciprocal teaching, the teacher and students have the opportunity to share "fix-up" strategies to construct meaning.

Most students can easily identify words that they need help deciphering. I often model how to figure out a difficult word and call on volunteers to share such words and how they figured them out. We also may work through a word together by discussing known word chunks and sounds and the context around the word. If your students are reluctant to admit that any vocabulary has caused them problems, a good strategy is to ask them to find a word that they figured out but that might be difficult for a younger child. Then, ask them to tell the class how they would teach the word to the younger child. Sometimes, this technique increases student participation when a class is first starting to learn about clarifying.

The language of clarifying may include the following prompts:

Identifying the problem

I didn't understand the part where...

This [sentence, paragraph, page, chapter] is not clear.

This doesn't make sense.

I can't figure out...

This is a tricky word because...

Clarifying strategies

To clarify an idea	*To clarify a word*
I reread the parts that I didn't understand.	I reread.
I read on to look for clues.	I look for word parts that I know.
I think about what I know.	I try to blend the sounds together.
I talk to a friend.	I think of another word that looks like this word.
	I read on to find clues.
	I try another word that makes sense.

The clarifying step of reciprocal teaching makes problem solving during reading more explicit for students. When they learn to identify and clarify difficult words or confusing portions of text, students become more strategic readers.

Summarizing

Summarizing is a complex process that requires the orchestration of various skills and strategies. To summarize effectively, students must recall and arrange in order only the important events in a text. The summary organization is based on the type of text—either narrative or expository (Lipson, 1996). When summarizing a story, students may use the setting, characters, problem, events, and resolution to guide their summaries. A nonfiction text requires them to determine important points and arrange them in a logical order.

During reciprocal teaching, the teacher and students take turns modeling summarizing. Students may use the following prompts to guide their summaries:

The most important ideas in this text are...

This part was about...

This book was about...

First,...

Next,...

Then,...

Finally,...

The story takes place...

The main characters are...

A problem occurs when...

Summarizing is extremely important because evidence exists that practice in summarizing improves students' reading comprehension of fiction and nonfiction alike, helping them construct an overall understanding of a text, story, chapter, or article (Rinehart, Stahl, & Erickson, 1986; Taylor, 1982). In reciprocal teaching lessons, students are provided with frequent opportunities to witness others summarizing and to participate in creating their own summaries, which helps them become more proficient readers.

Overcoming Obstacles When Implementing Reciprocal Teaching

Although study results indicate that students benefit from instruction using reciprocal teaching (see Introduction for examples), teachers may encounter some common problems when implementing the strategies in their classrooms. Figure 3 lists some of these problems—such as students struggling to use the strategies, creating a noisy classroom, and becoming bored with the strategies—and their possible solutions. Teachers also can anticipate difficulties with a specific reciprocal teaching strategy and overcome them with the suggestions provided in Figure 4.

In addition to providing students with the appropriate prompts and being aware of the problems that they may have with each strategy, reciprocal teaching instruction should include the following four instructional foundations: scaffolding, think-alouds, metacognition, and cooperative learning. Keep these building blocks in mind when introducing and extending reciprocal teaching lessons in any setting from whole-class groupings to literature circles.

Figure 3
Problems That Teachers May Encounter With Reciprocal Teaching and Suggested Solutions

Problem	Solution
Your students are not able to employ all four reciprocal teaching strategies easily.	• Use teacher modeling to introduce reciprocal teaching. Frequent teacher modeling is necessary. • You and your students can participate in think-alouds during which students explain how and why each strategy is helping them read.
You are not sure how to assess your students' progress.	• Observe your students' verbal responses. • Ask students to write brief individual responses for each strategy, or have a group collaborate on a response. • To assess individual progress, call on any student in the group to share, or collect written responses.

(continued)

Adapted from Hacker, D.J., & Tenent, A. (2002). Implementing reciprocal teaching in the classroom: Overcoming obstacles and making modifications. *Journal of Educational Psychology, 94*(4), 699–718.
Reciprocal Teaching at Work: Strategies for Improving Reading Comprehension by Lori D. Oczkus © 2003. Newark, DE: International Reading Association. May be copied for classroom use.

Figure 3 (continued)
Problems That Teachers May Encounter With Reciprocal Teaching and Suggested Solutions

Problem	Solution
Even with teacher modeling, your students still are not employing the strategies on their own.	• Scaffold students' progress through teacher or peer models, and have students take turns using the strategies. Allow for this constant turn-taking for the strategy to work well. • Ask students to verbalize why each strategy is important. Metacognition will aid them in using the strategies when they read on their own.
The classroom sometimes is noisy during reciprocal teaching lessons.	• Reciprocal teaching does require discussion and a certain amount of noise, but instruct students on how to work together quietly. • Circulate around the room to observe and listen in on groups. Call on groups to perform for the class and model quiet discussions.
You feel that you do not have enough time for reciprocal teaching strategies.	• Find time by weaving the strategies throughout the day into reading and content area lessons. Once students are familiar with the four strategies, you can fit them into lessons you are already teaching. • Use reciprocal teaching at least two to three times per week in any combination of settings in order to see results.
Your struggling readers are having trouble using reciprocal teaching strategies with peers in grade-level material.	• Try meeting with struggling readers several times a week to practice the strategies. Meet as an intervention group consistently all year if possible.
Your students are having trouble using the four strategies in longer texts.	• Start by using small chunks of text, such as a few paragraphs, and try gradually increasing the chunks of text used during reciprocal teaching lessons to pages, lessons, and eventually entire chapters.
Reciprocal teaching has become boring for the students and/or the teacher.	• Do not use paragraph-by-paragraph teacher-led lessons all the time. • Use the lessons in this book, which have dozens of applications for varying the delivery and setting for reciprocal teaching. • Include in your lessons other reading comprehension strategies such as making connections to prior knowledge and responding to literature.

Figure 4
Overcoming the Difficulties That Students Experience With Reciprocal Teaching Strategies

Common Problems Students Have With...	Try...
Predicting • making imaginative predictions that are not based on textual clues • not returning to predictions after reading to check their accuracy • predicting awkwardly with expository text	• modeling predictions by using think-alouds and textual clues • inviting the discussion director of small reciprocal teaching groups (see chapter 4) to return to predictions after reading to check their accuracy • asking students to preview illustrations and headings and think about what they believe they will learn from an expository text
Questioning • asking only literal or superficial questions • not asking any inferential questions	• continuously modeling higher-level questions that require using textual clues and prior knowledge • providing question starters • asking students to read the material and write several questions before meeting with a group • asking partners to alternate roles—one student reads aloud and the other asks a question • having students first read the material silently while hunting for questions, then read the material aloud before writing questions to answer and discuss
Clarifying • skipping the clarifying step altogether because they think there is nothing to clarify • clarifying words, not ideas • letting the teacher do all the clarifying	• modeling words and ideas to clarify • explicit teacher modeling of how to clarify ideas • using the Clarifying Bookmarks (see page 95) • asking students to circle or write words and/or sentences to clarify
Summarizing • giving summaries that are word-by-word retellings of the text • providing summaries that miss main points • rarely including main themes in summaries • not liking to summarize because it is difficult for them	• having students work in groups on other strategies but work as a class to contribute to a teacher-guided summary • asking groups to write a summary to share with the class for comments and ideas for revision, then having them rewrite and share again • having groups write and share summaries, and asking the class to vote for the strongest summary • getting at deeper themes by asking students to write letters to you or a classmate telling what they learned from the book • trying the "clear" summary minilesson (page 182) or the movie clips or freeze frames lesson (page 116) • making the summarizer task fun by having a student be a "reporter," using a microphone or drawing a quick sketch on a whiteboard or sheet of paper

Adapted from Hacker, D.J., & Tenent, A. (2002). Implementing reciprocal teaching in the classroom: Overcoming obstacles and making modifications. *Journal of Educational Psychology, 94*(4), 699–718.
Reciprocal Teaching at Work: Strategies for Improving Reading Comprehension by Lori D. Oczkus © 2003. Newark, DE: International Reading Association. May be copied for classroom use.

Scaffolding

Scaffolding reading instruction is similar to teaching a child how to ride a bicycle. First, the child watches people bicycle riding to get the idea and motivation for his or her own riding skills. Then, the parent holds on to the bicycle's seat and guides the child for a time. Eventually, the parent lets go of the seat but remains nearby (possibly even running next to the bicycle) in case support is needed. Finally, the child pedals away on his or her own.

During reciprocal teaching, the instruction is scaffolded, or supported. The students can see models of the four strategies, experience some "seat holding" as they try out reciprocal teaching in a supported environment, and, finally, work independently as they read while using reciprocal teaching strategies to help them comprehend the text. Every time students are engaged in reciprocal teaching, each has the opportunity to participate in scaffolded instruction because modeling and support are integral steps of the reciprocal teaching model. Therefore, students are propelled to the next reading level as the support that they receive guides them through more difficult texts and reading tasks.

Think-Alouds

Reciprocal teaching is not a pencil-and-paper activity. It was designed as a discussion technique in which think-alouds play an integral part. During a reciprocal teaching think-aloud, the reader talks aloud about each of the four strategies. Think-alouds show students what a good reader is thinking while reading, which again provides scaffolding toward developing good reading comprehension.

The steps to reading comprehension are less tangible than, say, the steps to a math problem, so this type of instruction may be new to teachers and students alike. Successful reciprocal teaching gives students ongoing opportunities to witness and conduct think-alouds using the four strategies. The teacher should not introduce reciprocal teaching and then abandon the modeling. Instead, think-alouds should occur every time students engage in reciprocal teaching lessons, and they should be conducted by both the teacher and students, who can take turns verbalizing the use of the reciprocal teaching strategies. This method allows students to see more clearly the steps to creating understanding while reading.

Metacognition

Metacognition is the awareness of one's own thinking processes. The think-aloud process goes hand in hand with metacognition as students talk about their thinking and how they are using predictions, questions, clarifications, and summaries. As the teacher, you can lead your students by sharing how the strategies have helped you comprehend a given text.

A discussion rich with metacognitive thinking will include student comments such as the following:

Prediction helped me the most today because it got me interested in the reading.

Clarifying helped me figure out the word *citizen* because I thought of the word *city*, and I reread the sentence to see what made sense.

Summarizing helped me remember all the important events in the story.

I had to reread the book to get the main idea so I could ask a question.

Metacognition is an integral component in reciprocal teaching because students learn to consciously think about and reflect on their strategy use. Ultimately, all students are trained to employ the same strategies that good readers use when monitoring their reading comprehension, and, therefore, students improve their own comprehension.

Cooperative Learning

The National Reading Panel (2000) recommends cooperative learning for improved reading comprehension, especially in content area texts. Because reciprocal teaching is intended to be a discussion technique, cooperative learning is integral to it. Reciprocal teaching builds on the cooperative nature of learning that causes one's reading comprehension to be deepened through social interactions.

The cooperative nature of reciprocal teaching is an important part of the scaffolded instruction, think-alouds, and metacognition inherent to reciprocal teaching lessons. Even when I teach whole-class lessons, I incorporate quick activities throughout the lesson that require students to turn to a partner in order to engage the students in more cooperative learning practice. Cooperative learning also occurs when students and teachers think aloud during discussions and their metacognition is made public. The following are some specific examples of cooperative learning in various classroom settings: If the class is reading a social studies text, I may model a summary of a portion of it and ask partners to work together to create a summary for the next section. When reading a novel as a class, groups of students each may be assigned a strategy to report on to the class. Even during guided reading group sessions, I might have pairs ask each other their questions after reading. Cooperative learning is, of course, already in place during literature circles, where students may work together to construct a recording sheet that includes their group members' collaborative efforts for a prediction, question, clarification, and summary.

What Reciprocal Teaching Does Not Accomplish

Although reciprocal teaching touches on four important strategies that students will use almost every time they read, students also need instruction in interacting with the text through personal connections, connections to other books, and connections to the broader world around them (Keene & Zimmermann, 1997). Depending on the text selection, the teacher may activate the students' prior knowledge or may need to supply some background information before reading to help them understand the text better. Good readers also visualize as they read and comprehend, and students may need further assistance in this important reading strategy. Many texts also require and invite the reader to make an aesthetic response to reading (Rosenblatt, 1978). Rich classroom discussions in which students have opportunities to react personally and emotionally to the reading, to express their opinions of the text, and to evaluate the text are extremely valuable in teaching reading. Discussion of the author's craft, the theme of the piece, or controversial issues addressed in text are all critical to helping students to comprehend text. If reading instruction were to focus only on the four reciprocal teaching strategies, teachers would miss out on important opportunities to build students' reading comprehension based on many of the humorous, interesting, and emotional responses that students have to what they read. It is through these types of aesthetic responses that teachers often are able to motivate students to love reading.

Figure 5
Books on Reciprocal Teaching or With Lessons That Strengthen Reciprocal Teaching
---

Cooper, J.D., Boschken, I., McWilliams, J., & Pistochini, L. (1999). *Soar to success: The intermediate intervention program*. Boston: Houghton Mifflin.

Hoyt, L. (1999). *Revisit, reflect, retell: Strategies for improving reading comprehension*. Portsmouth, NH: Heinemann.

Hoyt, L. (2002). *Make it real: Strategies for success with informational texts*. Portsmouth, NH: Heinemann.

Lubliner, S. (2001). *A practical guide to reciprocal teaching*. Bothell, WA: Wright Group.

McLaughlin, M., & Allen, M.B. (2002). *Guided comprehension: A teaching model for grades 3–8*. Newark, DE: International Reading Association.

McLaughlin, M., & Allen, M.B. (2002). *Guided comprehension in action: Lessons for grades 3–8*. Newark, DE: International Reading Association.

Reciprocal teaching is a wonderful tool that educators can use as part of their repertoire of reading comprehension strategies, but they also should teach scaffolded lessons on other strategies that students will need to become successful, lifelong readers (see the list of general reading comprehension books in Figure 1 on page 5). Figure 5 offers a list of books on reciprocal teaching and that contain lessons on reciprocal teaching for further reference.

Assessment Options for Reciprocal Teaching

Assessment tools for reciprocal teaching include the observation of students during discussions and some occasional, brief written responses using the four reciprocal teaching strategies.

What to look for (see the rubric in Appendix A on page 195)

- student use of each strategy
- orchestrated use of all four strategies
- ability to define each strategy and explain how it helps with reading comprehension (see also Appendix C on page 203)

How to help students

- teach the minilessons at the end of each chapter to small groups or the whole class

CHAPTER SUMMARY

- Reciprocal teaching, when used consistently, can produce rapid results and growth in comprehension for readers of all ages (Cooper et al., 2000; Palincsar & Brown, 1984).

- Four strategies used by good readers—predicting, questioning, clarifying, and summarizing—are employed in any order during reciprocal teaching sessions.

- Predicting helps students anticipate events, actions, and problems in the text.

- Questioning is important because good readers self-question before, during, and after reading.

- Clarifying assists students in identifying problems or areas of confusion as they read and offers ways to solve the problems.

- Summarizing is a complex skill that requires students to select and arrange in order only the most important points from the text. Evidence exists that, when students are taught to summarize, their reading comprehension improves.

- When attempting to implement reciprocal teaching, teachers also may face common obstacles (see Figure 3 on page 19).

- Students may encounter some common difficulties as they work through the strategies (refer to Figure 4 on page 21).

- The building blocks to successful reciprocal teaching instruction are scaffolded instruction, think-alouds performed by the teacher and students, metacognition, and cooperative learning.

- Reciprocal teaching, although very effective, does not stand alone. Its four strategies are part of a broader comprehension framework of skills and strategies that should be modeled for and taught to students. Other important comprehension strategies include visualizing, making connections, and evaluating, or making judgments (Keene & Zimmermann, 1997; McLaughlin & Allen, 2002; Pearson et al., 1992).

Reflections for Group Study, Self-Study, or Staff Development

1 Describe each reciprocal teaching strategy and explain how each helps readers to understand text. How do the strategies work together as a package? In what order should you teach them?

2 What are some language prompts that you can use with your students to get them started with reciprocal teaching strategies?

3 List some common obstacles that teachers encounter when implementing reciprocal teaching. How can you anticipate and overcome them?

4 List some common problems that students may have with each strategy. How can you assist your students with these problems?

5 How will you address your students' problem areas and reinforce their strengths?

6 Why does reciprocal teaching not stand alone? What other important strategies should be part of a comprehensive reading comprehension program?

7 What are the four important building blocks that must be in place in order for reciprocal teaching to be successful? Explain how each foundation works to create an environment for learning.

8 Demonstrate a sample think-aloud using one of the strategies.

9 Name some assessment tools that you can use to evaluate student progress in the four strategies.

CHAPTER 2

RECIPROCAL TEACHING
in Whole-Class Sessions

I like questioning because it gives me a chance to look back and really think about what I read. Questioning makes me feel more grown up because I get to ask questions. It makes me feel like I'm interviewing someone.

—*Robbie, grade 3*

Description of Reciprocal Teaching in Whole-Class Sessions

When structured properly, the whole-class session can provide students with a sense of community and support that reinforces the reciprocal teaching strategies. Reciprocal teaching in a whole-class session also offers students a place to establish a common language for the four strategies and affords all students the opportunity to participate in the same piece of literature. When working with the whole class, you initially can scaffold reciprocal teaching instruction and then use cooperative groups, pairs, or guided reading groups for a follow-up lesson. Using whole-class instruction to bring the class together for meaningful activities before and after reading allows your students to benefit from the rich backgrounds and ideas of their classmates.

I find that when my students and I meet as a whole class, they have a sense of community, of being in a place where they feel that they are cared about and valued (Kohn, 1996). As the students and I work through a text, we form a common bond and share an experience. The message to my students of all ability levels is that I believe they are capable of reading, understanding what they read, and sharing ideas surrounding the literature or content area text. I have worked with many struggling readers who appreciate being included in class work with grade-level literature, and their comments are insightful and respected by their classmates. When I conduct a class demonstration of reciprocal teaching strategies, I cannot always tell which students struggle and frequently am surprised after the lesson when the classroom teacher tells me who they are because these students often shine in whole-class sessions. When we as teachers use a common piece of nonfiction or fiction with our students in a whole-class session, we are providing an engaging experience for all of them, regardless of ability level.

Whole-class instruction can be an effective setting in which to introduce and reinforce reciprocal teaching strategies. However, when the whole-class session is used alongside other groupings, including guided reading groups and literature circles, it has some disadvantages that you should keep in mind. A common drawback is that individual students have many diverse needs that cannot all be met in a whole-class session. For example, some children are not attentive during whole-class sessions and need a small-group format to absorb what they are learning. Other students may be shy and reluctant to speak during whole-class sessions. However, an intuitive teacher will sense during a whole-class session when it is time to shift gears and break into cooperative groups, independent work, literacy centers, or a teacher-led group. By mixing whole-class instruction with other groupings and using engaging whole-class techniques, you can overcome the challenges that whole-class teaching presents.

This chapter outlines essential teaching foundations that facilitate and enhance whole-class instruction, whether you are introducing or reinforcing reciprocal teaching strategies. In fact, every lesson in this book can be converted fairly easily into a whole-class lesson if you choose to do so. (See Figure 6 for an overview of the lessons presented in this chapter.) Each lesson includes the essential elements for successful

Figure 6
Lesson Overview Chart: Reciprocal Teaching in Whole-Class Sessions

Lesson	Pages	Description
Introducing the Reciprocal Teaching Team—The Fabulous Four	39 to 48	A think-aloud lesson with characters and voices to make reciprocal teaching strategies come alive
Using the Be the Teacher Bookmark	49 to 53	A bookmark and lesson with prompts for students to predict, question, clarify, and summarize
Using Cooperative Table Groups	54 to 58	A guided practice lesson with cooperative groups and a fun reciprocal teaching puzzle
Using Different Types of Reading Materials	59 to 66	Teaching tips and considerations for using reciprocal teaching with different kinds of reading materials
Minilesson: What's Your Prediction?	67	Student-made predictions shared with others in a stroll line
Minilesson: Pick a Question	68	Student pairs asking questions about a text, using question words that they draw from a hat
Minilesson: Clarifying With the *Independent Strategies* Poem	69 to 70	Students learning about word-level clarification strategies as they participate in a shared reading
Minilesson: Table Group Summaries	71	Table groups summarizing portions of the text, with the class assembling each group's contribution for a complete summary

scaffolding through teacher modeling and student participation. I recommend that you reinforce the reciprocal teaching strategies throughout the day during whole-class literature lessons and content area reading after your class is familiar with them.

Goals of Reciprocal Teaching During Whole-Class Sessions

The goals of using reciprocal teaching during whole-class sessions are

- to establish a common language for using reciprocal teaching strategies,

- to increase opportunities to teach and scaffold reciprocal teaching strategies,

- to guide students of all reading levels to improve their reading comprehension in grade-level material,

- to show students how to use multiple strategies to comprehend what they read,

- to engage in reading comprehension discussions using the reciprocal teaching strategies, and

- to provide a community format for reinforcing the routines and procedures used in guided reading groups and literature circles.

Incorporating the Whole-Class Session With Other Settings

One way to create community among student readers is to begin a reciprocal teaching lesson with the whole class, then move to a type of flexible grouping, and, finally, return to the whole-class session for sharing and reflection (Opitz, 1998). For example, I used a whole-class session to work through an introduction to and scaffold instruction in reciprocal teaching strategies with a fourth-grade class reading the nonfiction book *Sunken Treasure* (Gibbons, 1998). First, I activated the students' prior knowledge by asking them what they knew about lost ships or sunken treasure. After we had a discussion and filled in the "What We Know About" section of a Know-Want-Learn chart (Ogle, 1986; see page 98 for an example), we previewed the illustrations and came up with some questions that the students had about the topic. I also read several pages of the book aloud and modeled the four reciprocal teaching strategies in a think-aloud. Then, I asked the students to work in pairs to read the selection, stopping every two pages to work through reciprocal teaching strategies. During the partner reading time, I met briefly with two guided reading groups that each had a majority of struggling readers (see chapter 3 for discussion of using reciprocal teaching with guided reading groups), and I used reciprocal teaching in this small, teacher-led group format. The groups of six students each were organized around needs and were flexible as those needs changed. About once a month, I used assessments in which students either wrote or verbalized their use of the four reciprocal teaching strategies. During our regular sessions, once the students finished with a reading assignment, the whole class convened to contribute to the "What We Learned" column of the Know-Want-Learn chart and to discuss their reactions to the book. I also asked the students to reflect on how each reciprocal teaching strategy had helped them understand what they had read. The students demonstrated an understanding of the text and remembered what they read as they wrote their reflection on what they had learned.

In general, teachers weave in and out of whole-class instruction for different purposes. Figure 7 outlines some instances when whole-class instruction may be implemented to enhance your reciprocal teaching lessons.

Essential Foundations for Effective Whole-Class Instruction

For reciprocal teaching to be effective, regardless of the classroom setting used, certain instructional foundations—such as scaffolding, think-alouds, metacognition, and cooperative learning—must be in place. (Refer to chapter 1 for a discussion of these terms.)

Scaffolding during whole-class lessons includes teacher modeling, student participation, and reflection on strategy use. You might open the scaffolded minilesson by stating the reason for the lesson, such as "I am going to show you how I use the four reciprocal teaching strategies to help me understand what I am reading when I read a newspaper article." Then, you can continue by reading aloud from the article, modeling what you are thinking for each strategy. As you proceed, invite student pairs or groups to take turns trying out the four reciprocal teaching strategies and

Figure 7
Implementing Whole-Class Sessions and Other Classroom Settings

Whole-Class Session Whole Class—Partners or Table Groups—Whole Class	• Have all students read a common piece of literature or nonfiction. • Introduce, model, and reinforce reciprocal teaching strategies in content area reading. • Have students reflect on learning and use of strategies. • Ask tables or partners to discuss responses before they share with the whole class.
Whole-Class Session and Guided Reading Groups Whole Class—Guided Reading Groups—Whole Class	• Introduce the whole class to the same piece of literature, including background and vocabulary. • Lead guided reading groups through a reading of the selection. • Bring the whole class together to discuss the reading. • Alternatively, have the whole class read a common text and have guided reading groups each read a related text at the appropriate instructional reading level.
Whole-Class Session and Literature Circles Whole Class—Literature Circles—Whole Class	• Introduce, reinforce, or reflect on reciprocal teaching strategies, literature circle procedures, and trouble shooting with the whole class. • With your students, model literature circles using reciprocal teaching. • Have students return to a whole-class format to report their understandings and findings.

have them reflect on how the strategies help them understand the text. End the lesson with students reading on their own to practice predicting, questioning, clarifying, and summarizing. Reciprocal teaching is unique in having a design that naturally includes scaffolding by either the teacher or student peers every time it is used in the classroom.

Think-alouds also are inherent in reciprocal teaching, and they are an important foundation for achieving maximum results in reading comprehension. Each reciprocal teaching session includes opportunities for both the teacher and the students to make their thinking public. Because reading strategies are not as visible as, say, strategies involved in a science experiment, it is critical to talk through the steps and the thought processes involved in comprehending a text so good reading strategies become more tangible for students. Think-alouds are tied to scaffolding as the teacher models by thinking aloud about his or her own use of the strategies, using a text that the students also have in front of them. After the teacher's think-aloud, he or she can invite the students to share their thinking as they use the strategies in the text. By witnessing constant think-alouds conducted by the teacher and their peers, students begin to internalize the reciprocal teaching strategies and employ them during independent reading.

Another necessary instructional foundation is metacognition, which is easily reinforced during whole-class sessions. Throughout the school day, you can lead minilessons involving metacognition by using reciprocal teaching strategies for one or two pages in a content area chapter or when your students are reading a newspaper article. During the minilessons, model your thinking aloud, then ask your students to practice asking one another questions based on the text and explaining their thinking. Consider the power of talking about the four strategies—predict, question, clarify, and summarize—throughout the school day. Talking about the four reciprocal teaching strategies throughout the school day is a powerful tool to enhance your students' ability to use metacognition.

Cooperative learning is also important for keeping the students engaged during a whole-class session. All teachers have had the experience when teaching the whole class of having only the same handful of students raising their hands to respond (Routman, 2002). To avoid this pitfall of whole-class instruction, ask your students to turn to a partner to practice or discuss a point in your lesson. Also, weave table groups—in which students work with others who sit at their tables—or cooperative groups—in which students are placed in mixed-ability or interest groups—throughout the lesson for variety. The cooperative atmosphere of the combination of whole-class and small-group exercises encourages every child to respond to and think about the lesson. And when student involvement in the lesson increases, so does student achievement (Routman, 2002).

In addition to using the four instructional foundations of scaffolding, think-alouds, metacognition, and cooperative learning in your reciprocal teaching lessons, using props and visuals can help engage your students in the lessons and make their learning more memorable. I suggest posting the four reciprocal teaching strategies in the classroom where all students can see them and where you can easily refer to them during whole-class sessions. Also, it is helpful if every student has access to a personal reference to the strategies. You can give the Be the Teacher

Bookmark (page 53) to every student to use during reciprocal teaching lessons. Using simple visuals such as these can involve your students in a lesson that helps make the learning stick.

Overall, using reciprocal teaching during whole-class sessions strengthens comprehension by

- scaffolding student learning with teacher modeling, think-alouds, metacognition, and cooperative learning;
- modeling and practicing reciprocal teaching strategies as a multiple strategy package;
- focusing on one reciprocal teaching strategy at a time during minilessons;
- guiding students through content area and other grade-level reading;
- creating an environment of community in which all students are expected to participate; and
- setting the expectation that all students will use reciprocal teaching to improve their comprehension.

Figure 8 outlines some instances when you may decide to choose a whole-class session as the most effective way to provide reciprocal teaching instruction.

The Big Picture in Whole-Class Sessions: What Else You Will Need to Do

The best advice in regard to whole-class sessions is to avoid overdoing them. Although there is some security in providing the same instruction to all your students, educators know that students need other types of groupings—both student- and teacher-led—to meet their diverse needs. Partners or groups are effective because when students talk about their thinking with one another, their learning increases, plus you can avoid the common pitfall of only a few students raising their hands to participate in whole-class discussions.

You also need to ensure that every student responds during whole-class sessions. The responses can be in the form of a written assignment, a partner activity or discussion, or a cooperative group peer discussion. There are many ways to involve students during your lessons. For

Figure 8
When to Use Whole-Class Sessions

Work With the Whole Class to...	Lessons and Materials for the Whole Class
Introduce Reciprocal Teaching Strategies	**Lessons** • Introducing the Reciprocal Teaching Team—The Fabulous Four • Using the Be the Teacher Bookmark on page 53 **Materials** • At first, use books or articles that are easier than grade level or short. • Use props for each character.
Introduce a New Reading Selection • Build students' background knowledge and/or activate their prior knowledge. • Introduce and build selection vocabulary. • Model the four reciprocal teaching strategies.	**Lessons** • Use lessons from any chapter of this book. **Materials** • Use core literature or content area texts.
Troubleshoot Any Problems With Reciprocal Teaching • Identify and address problems with a particular strategy.	**Lessons** • Use minilessons from this or any other chapter. **Materials** • These will vary depending on the lessons used.
Reflect on Reciprocal Teaching Strategies • Think aloud and discuss how each strategy enhanced your reading comprehension.	**Lessons** • Try reflection suggestions found in the assessment portion of each lesson in this book. • Ask, How did each strategy help you today? Which strategy helped you the most, and why? **Materials** • These will vary depending on the lessons used.
Model Procedures • Guide students who are having problems in literature circles, table groups, or pairs.	**Lessons** • Ask volunteers to model reciprocal teaching strategies for the group. Discuss the modeling with the class. • Call on a group member to report successes and problems with their groups.

example, after modeling a prediction using a think-aloud, pause and invite student pairs to turn to each other and try predicting before you move on to the next strategy. Then, continue by repeating these steps for another strategy. As options, you may pause periodically for students to work in teams to provide written responses to the strategy or have pairs

---

Figure 9
Books on Flexible Grouping and With Suggestions for Whole-Class Lessons

Caldwell, J., & Ford, M.P. (2002). *Where have all the bluebirds gone? How to soar with flexible grouping.* Portsmouth, NH: Heinemann.

Opitz, M.F. (1998). *Flexible grouping in reading: Practical ways to help all students become better readers.* New York: Scholastic.

Routman, R. (2002). *Reading essentials: The specifics you need to teach reading well.* Portsmouth, NH: Heinemann.

---

or groups discuss how a particular strategy helped them gain a better understanding of the text. By using the Be the Teacher Bookmark on page 53 or a wall poster of the reciprocal teaching strategies, you can involve your students in whole-class lessons with prompts for the strategies.

Chapters 3 and 4 have many suggestions for using small-group formats such as guided reading groups and literature circles for instructing students on reciprocal teaching strategies. By combining the best of what whole-class instruction has to offer with small-group activities, you can be sure that all your students' needs are met. See Figure 9 for other books that discuss flexible class groupings and offer suggestions for whole-class lessons.

Assessment Options for Reciprocal Teaching During Whole-Class Sessions

When you use reciprocal teaching strategies with your whole class, there are several simple assessment and observation points that can guide future instruction. Refer to the reciprocal teaching rubric in Appendix A (page 195) for detailed guidelines on what to look for when observing students engaging in a reciprocal teaching discussion. The following list provides general guidelines for student observation:

- Listen to the students who respond during whole-class sessions. Are they effectively using the four reciprocal teaching strategies?

- During whole-class sessions, provide time for table groups to work cooperatively. Circulate around the room and listen to the students' interactions. Intervene when necessary to model a strategy or coach individual students. Pull aside groups that are having trouble with a particular strategy, and teach them the appropriate minilesson from the end of this chapter (pages 67–71).

- Allow time for student pairs to interact and try the reciprocal teaching strategies. Listen for their effective use of the strategies, and assist pairs who are having trouble. For struggling students, model a think-aloud using one or all of the strategies.

- Create a brief written assessment by asking students to fill in the Literature Discussion Sheet for Reciprocal Teaching (page 141) either cooperatively, with one student serving as recorder for the group, or individually. Students should not be asked to write the strategies early in reciprocal teaching instruction, but after a few lessons have them complete the written record to guide your future instruction. You might use the form every two weeks rather than in every discussion.

- After meeting in groups or pairs, pull the whole class together again and point out specific examples of students who used reciprocal teaching strategies effectively. Share what those students discussed, and allow for all students to try again.

- Lead a class discussion on each reciprocal teaching strategy. Ask your students to define each strategy and identify what steps are involved. Record their responses on a piece of butcher paper or a whiteboard.

Lesson 1: Introducing the Reciprocal Teaching Team—The Fabulous Four

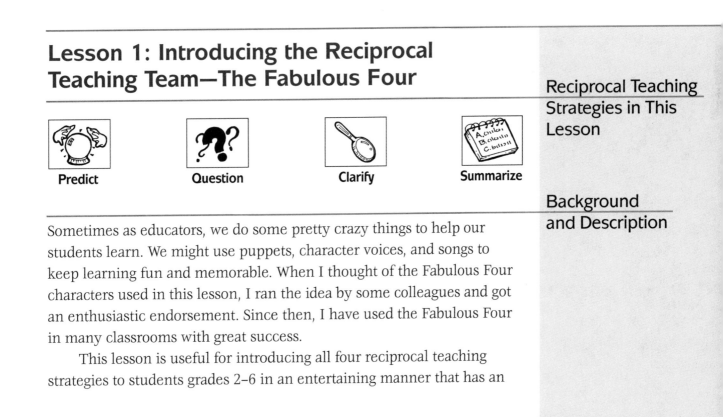

Predict **Question** **Clarify** **Summarize**

Reciprocal Teaching Strategies in This Lesson

Background and Description

Sometimes as educators, we do some pretty crazy things to help our students learn. We might use puppets, character voices, and songs to keep learning fun and memorable. When I thought of the Fabulous Four characters used in this lesson, I ran the idea by some colleagues and got an enthusiastic endorsement. Since then, I have used the Fabulous Four in many classrooms with great success.

This lesson is useful for introducing all four reciprocal teaching strategies to students grades 2–6 in an entertaining manner that has an impact during a brief demonstration. The lesson shows students how reciprocal teaching strategies work together and separately while someone is reading a text.

The goal of the lesson is to introduce students to all four strategies by having them watch the strategies in use during a teacher think-aloud. If you are a bit shy, you can use either the characters' voices or the props; otherwise, you can use both simultaneously. After this initial lesson, you might not use the characters again, but you might refer to them as you continue modeling the strategies while thinking aloud. How far you will want to take the reciprocal teaching characters depends on your students and their interest in the characters. A brief description of the characters follows:

Peter (or Madam) the Powerful Predictor
Two different characters can be used for the role of the Powerful Predictor—either a weightlifter with an Arnold Schwarzenegger–like voice or a fortuneteller. You should choose whichever character better suits your students' interests. The Schwarzenegger character, Peter the Powerful Predictor, needs small handweights as props. For the fortuneteller, Madam Powerful Predictor, use a flowing scarf and colorful, beaded necklaces as props.

Quincy the Quizzical Questioner
Quincy is a fast-talking game show host who sports a necktie, sports coat, and plastic microphone (preferably, the kind that echoes). Quincy usually begins his part of the lesson by shouting out, "Who, what, when, where, why, how, and what if? I am Quincy the Quizzical Questioner. I ask questions before, during, and after reading."

Clara the Careful Clarifier
Clara is a sophisticated lady who wears white gloves, reading glasses, and a pointer. She uses phrases such as "Yes, darling" and "That would be quite lovely" throughout the lesson. She often holds the reading material very close to her face as she tries to clarify a word or reread a portion of text for understanding.

Sammy the Super Summarizer
There are two choices for the summarizer character. Sammy can be either a cowboy with a cowboy hat and a lasso, rounding up the main idea—"I am Sammy the Super Summarizer, and I round up the main ideas and summarize anything I read"—or a sunglasses-wearing robot

with a mechanical voice—"I ...am...Sammy...the Super...Summarizer...I summarize...to help...me understand...what I...am reading."

The Fabulous Four can be fun to use in many different classrooms to introduce reciprocal teaching strategies to students in a creative way. In the classes that I have taught, students seem to more easily remember the reciprocal teaching strategies and how they help readers when I use this rather comical lesson plan. (The Classroom Story on page 45 shows this lesson plan in action.)

Ideally, all the reciprocal teaching strategies work together as students read text. As a teacher, your temptation may be to teach the strategies one at a time and then introduce a new strategy as your students master the previous one. Unfortunately, that method does not model how good readers use these strategies. Good readers sample, rotate, and make constant use of all four strategies to make meaning from a text (Palincsar & Brown, 1984). Your goal is to help your students to feel the flow of using all four strategies together. Later, your lessons can focus on one strategy at a time to improve both your students' application of it and, ultimately, their reading comprehension.

As you model for your students how the four reciprocal teaching strategies can be used as reading comprehension tools, you should point out to them that there are other important reading comprehension strategies that good readers use. You want your students to be aware that reciprocal teaching strategies are part of a bigger framework of strategies and skills that good readers employ constantly (Keene & Zimmermann, 1997; McLaughlin & Allen, 2002; Pearson et al., 1992), so you might post a list of the broader comprehension strategies on the wall somewhere in the classroom for your students' reference.

Materials

- Reading material: Any text—a newspaper article, Big Book, or a fiction or nonfiction selection from a reading series—will work as long as students can see the text.

- Props for each character:
    Peter (or Madam) the Powerful Predictor: handweights, or a flowing scarf and colorful, beaded necklaces, respectively
    Quincy the Quizzical Questioner: a necktie, sports coat, and a plastic microphone (that echoes, if possible)
    Clara the Careful Clarifier: glasses, white gloves, and a pointer

Sammy the Super Summarizer: a rope lasso and a cowboy hat, or sunglasses

- An overhead projector, optional

Teacher Modeling

1. Brainstorm and chart strategies that good readers use. Ask your students what good readers do to understand what they read. Have pairs or table groups brainstorm ideas, and then list their responses on a piece of butcher paper or a whiteboard.

2. Share the objective of the lesson. Tell your students that today you will focus on four strategies that good readers use to comprehend text as they read and that you are going to introduce them to the strategies as characters who will think aloud.

3. Introduce each character. Your students will need to see the reading material you are using, so use either a Big Book or an article on an overhead projector, or make sure your students have copies of the book.

   Tell your students that each character will help you read the chosen text effectively and that you will be thinking aloud to model what a good reader thinks while trying to make meaning from a text. Throughout the lesson, model the reciprocal teaching strategies after reading small bits of text such as paragraphs or pages.

   - *Predictor*: Using either the Peter or the fortuneteller character, preview the text by looking at the title, author, covers, and several illustrations within the book. Model how to use clues from the text to make predictions. Use language such as "I previewed the title, cover, and illustrations, and using these clues, I predict that...."

   - *Questioner*: Wear the game show host attire of a sports coat and necktie, and use a plastic microphone as you model how to ask questions throughout the reading process. Show students how to ask questions before reading by previewing the text and wondering aloud what it is about.

     During the reading, stop periodically and say, "Here is a great spot where a teacher might ask a question. Let me reread the paragraph. I think a great question for this text might start with the question word *how."* Continue to pause and ask questions that check your understanding of the text. Also, model how to answer questions as you read.

- *Clarifier*: Role-playing as Clara the Careful Clarifier, choose a long or difficult word and pause to think aloud about how to decipher it based on chunks, sounds, meaning, and context. You also might choose an entire sentence or passage and think aloud how to reread (one of Clara's most useful strategies) to gather meaning.

- *Summarizer*: Choose which summarizer character voice you prefer—either the cowboy or the robot—to summarize the page or paragraph that you have read aloud. Demonstrate the value in rereading several times and in thinking about the main ideas to shrink material into a concise summary.

Student Participation

1. Reflect on the strategies. After your first reading and strategy modeling, ask your students what they noticed about each character. Ask questions such as, How did each character help me understand the reading? What did each character do or say? How could we use these strategies to help us understand what we read? List your students' responses on a piece of butcher paper or a whiteboard.

2. Guide your students to use the strategies themselves. Lead a guided discussion by asking your students which character they would like to see go first.

   Read aloud another segment of the text as you role-play, and invite students to help the character model his or her reciprocal teaching strategy. After each character models his or her think-aloud, have your students work in pairs to come up with additional predictions, questions, points or words to clarify, or summaries.

3. Have individual students or pairs draw the Fabulous Four characters. Instruct students to complete the Sketching the Fabulous Four Reciprocal Teaching Team form on page 48, drawing what they think every character looks like and then writing about what each character does.

   Students should write or discuss a reflection on how each strategy helps them to comprehend what they read. They may refer to the list

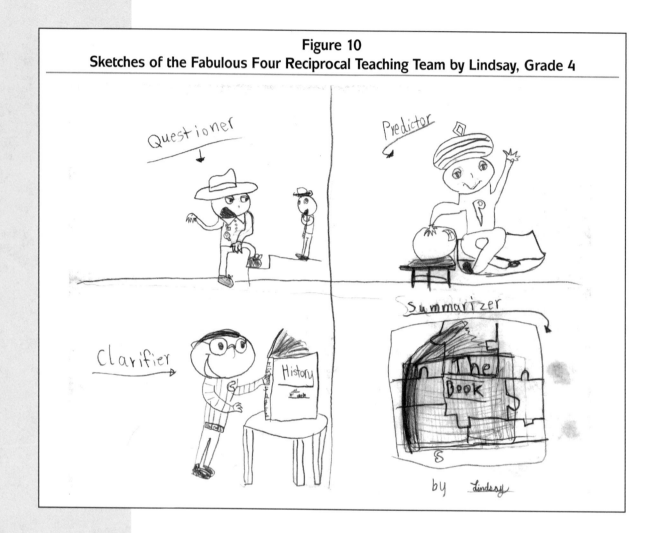

Figure 10
Sketches of the Fabulous Four Reciprocal Teaching Team by Lindsay, Grade 4

that the class has already created on the piece of butcher paper or whiteboard. Discuss, share, and then display on the classroom wall the reciprocal teaching characters that your students draw. See the student sample in Figure 10.

Assessment Tips

I recommend that you use several of the following informal assessments while engaging students in this lesson: Circulate around the classroom, and listen to pairs of students during the guided activity after your students have heard a model for a reciprocal teaching strategy. Do the pairs copy the model? Students may offer the same summary, for example, as yours. Copying is OK at this early stage if the students understood the model. The following points will help you determine whether your students understood.

- Do your students come up with a sensible but new prediction, question, point or word to clarify (or way to clarify the word that you modeled), or summary?
- Do the students' drawings reflect the character who uses the strategy during reading?
- Can your students verbalize to one another the jobs of each reciprocal teaching team member?

If your students are having difficulty verbalizing the jobs, drawing the characters, or giving their own examples for each strategy, consider teaching the minilessons (pp. 67–71) that separately reinforce each of the reciprocal teaching strategies. Also, use the suggestions found in Figure 4 (p. 21), Overcoming Difficulties That Students Experience With Reciprocal Teaching Strategies, when your students have problems using any of the four strategies.

Classroom Story

Introducing the Reciprocal Teaching Team—The Fabulous Four—to Grade 2

As I wait for the second graders to arrive after lunch, I check to see if I have all the props for my reciprocal teaching characters lesson. I always feel a little silly using voices and props to dramatize the strategy characters (especially in front of the teachers who watch me), but the effort is worth it. In the classrooms where I have tried this lesson, the students have caught on to the strategies a bit faster than when I have not used it. In this particular second-grade class, today is the first time that these students will be introduced to the reciprocal teaching model, even though their teacher has introduced some of the good reader strategies—previewing, self-questioning, making connections, visualizing, knowing how words work, monitoring, summarizing, and evaluating (Keene & Zimmermann, 1997; McLaughlin & Allen, 2002; Pearson et al., 1992)—and used them for four months. These students most likely will have some familiarity with the four reciprocal teaching strategies: predicting, questioning, clarifying, and summarizing.

Predicting   As the students gather at my feet on the rug next to my chair, I begin the lesson by telling them that they are about to meet four characters that help them to read every day. The book I have chosen to model from is the nonfiction text *Zipping, Zapping, Zooming Bats* (Earle, 1995). I begin, "Boys and girls, I'd like you to meet my friend Peter the Powerful Predictor." I bring out some small handweights and begin lifting them as I talk about making powerful predictions. I try to use an Arnold Schwarzenegger–like voice, which is difficult to maintain throughout the entire lesson, but all the kids know who he is and love it when I try. The students giggle as they watch in earnest to see what this "crazy lady" will do next.

Then, I show the book's cover and talk about the powerful predictions that I can make by using the book's captions and pictures. I conduct a brief preview of the book's first few pages by studying illustrations and headings to make predictions. "I predict for the first part of the book that I will learn how many insects some bats eat and how they use echolocation to catch their prey, yaaah," I model in my Austrian accent. Then, I ask the students to work with a partner to give at least two additional predictions, and we share our predictions in a whole-class setting.

Questioning   Next, I ask the students to close their eyes so I can introduce them to another character from the reciprocal teaching team—Quincy the Quizzical Questioner. I usually bring a plastic microphone that echoes and use an announcer voice for Quincy. "I am Quincy the Quizzical Questioner, and I have some questions as I read," I boom into the microphone. Then, I read aloud just four pages of the text as myself, and as I read I stop to be interrupted by Quincy: "Hey, why do bats chomp their weight in bugs? I wonder why the author chose to compare how much a bat eats to how many peanut butter and jelly sandwiches a human eats."

I ask the students to pair up again to look over the first four pages of the book, choose a page, and make up a question to ask the group. I tell them that they can ask a question that is answered in the text. The pairs are eager to share their questions:

"Why are bats good hunters?"
"How many insects does a gray bat eat in one night?"
"How many bats live in Bracken Cave in Texas?"

Clarifying   When I am finished alternating between reading and questioning for several pages, I stop and tell the students that there is another character they should meet—Clara the Careful Clarifier. For Clara's props, I have brought a pair of large glasses and a pointer. I choose a sophisticated accent and say, "Hello, children. I'm Clara the Careful Clarifier, and I am here to see if there are any words or parts in the story that I don't understand, darlings."

I look on page 8 of *Zipping, Zapping, Zooming Bats* and read, "'Together they *blank* 250 tons of insects every night.' The missing word starts with *m*, and I see a part that I know at the end—*unch*—which looks a bit like the word *lunch*. I put them together and get *munch*." I reread the sentence and tell the students that it makes sense, so I have successfully clarified a word. I tell them that the next time I visit the class, I may clarify a part of the text that does not make sense, instead of just one word.

Once again, I ask pairs of students to work together, this time to find a word that may need to be clarified. Pairs share their words and explain to the class how they deciphered them.

Summarizing   Finally, I tell the students that it is time for Sammy the Super Summarizer to pay them a visit. Today, I wear my cowboy hat and use a jump rope as a lasso that I twirl above my head.

Playing the cowboy, I say, "I'm rounding up the main idea, class. Watch this, I'm gonna reread the pages to myself quickly to get the information fresh in my head, then I will be ready to sum up the main idea!" I page through the text, mumbling various main points to myself. Then, I model a summary of the first few pages of the book:

> Bats are expert hunters that come out at night to hunt insects. Bats eat half their own weight in bugs, and some bats eat thousands of insects in one night. Bats won't hurt people but help them by eating unwanted insects that cause damage to crops.

Because summarizing can be so challenging, I invite the students to skim the same pages that I just summarized and then summarize them with a partner. I tell them that it is OK to copy my summary.

After all that modeling, I have the children go back to their desks and, using the Be the Teacher Bookmark, work with a partner through the next four pages of the book, stopping to predict, question, clarify, and summarize.

Reflection and Next Steps　　After I circulate around the room to listen to the student pairs, I conduct a whole-class discussion, asking students to review the four strategies and tell me what each character does to help us read. In the weeks to come, the classroom teacher and I will use a variety of techniques with reciprocal teaching and will model the strategies while using Big Books, articles, and short stories.

Sketching the Fabulous Four Reciprocal Teaching Team

The Predictor
Sketch what you think the predictor looks like. What does the predictor do?

The Questioner
Sketch what you think the questioner looks like. What does the questioner do?

The Clarifier
Sketch what you think the clarifier looks like. What does the clarifier do?

The Summarizer
Sketch what you think the summarizer looks like. What does the summarizer do?

Show your sketches to a partner, and explain to him or her how each character helps you understand what you read.

Lesson 2: Using the Be the Teacher Bookmark

Reciprocal Teaching Strategies in This Lesson

Predict

Question

Clarify

Summarize

Background and Description

The Be the Teacher Bookmark (see bookmark on page 53) has prompts for each reciprocal teaching strategy and can aid students as they work their way through texts and reciprocal teaching discussions. It is a useful tool not only in introductory lessons with reciprocal teaching but also as a guide throughout the school year every time you use reciprocal teaching strategies. You can apply this flexible teaching aid in a variety of settings, including whole-class sessions, partner interactions, guided reading groups, and literature circles. If you choose, you can print the bookmark in color and laminate it for attractiveness and durability. One second-grade teacher I know stores the laminated bookmarks in plastic bins at the centers of desk clusters. Because the bookmarks are easily accessible, she can ask students to grab their bookmarks anytime she weaves reciprocal teaching strategies into a shared reading or social studies lesson.

This lesson requires multiple strategy use—understanding that good readers use more than one strategy during a given reading—and emphasizes using think-alouds as an integral part of reciprocal teaching. Remind your students that there are other strategies that good readers use, such as previewing, making connections, and visualizing (Keene & Zimmermann, 1997; McLaughlin & Allen, 2002; Pearson et al., 1992).

Materials

- A Big Book or multiple copies of the teacher-chosen reading material
- A copy of the Be the Teacher Bookmark (laminated and in color, optional) for each student (see page 53)
- An overhead projector, optional

1. When introducing reciprocal teaching strategies to your students, ask them to tell you what good readers do and list those ideas on a chart that the whole class can see.

2. Pass out the Be the Teacher Bookmarks, and tell your students that you will model four strategies that good readers use to comprehend text effectively.

   Tell your students that the strategies will help them to better understand and remember what they read and that they will have the opportunity to think aloud and "be the teacher" after watching you demonstrate how.

3. Use a Big Book or hand out multiple copies of the chosen text so all your students can see it. If you are not using a Big Book, for effective modeling you might use an overhead projector copy of the same text that the students have in their hands. You may want to put the bookmark on the overhead projector as well.

4. Model for your students the use of all the prompts. First, predict by previewing the text's title, covers, headings, and illustrations. Next, read aloud a paragraph or two from the text.

   After reading, model a think-aloud using the other prompts on the reciprocal teaching bookmark—question, clarify, and summarize. You might end the think-aloud by predicting again what might happen in the next portion of the text.

5. Use the bookmark continually to model all four reciprocal teaching strategies during think-alouds. Over time, your students will become familiar with the language of the strategies and the multiple strategy use of reciprocal teaching.

6. After your students understand that reciprocal teaching strategies work together as tools for comprehending a text, you may want to focus on one strategy at a time while using the bookmark prompts and modeling a think-aloud. This modeling can be done in a whole-class, guided reading, or literature circle setting.

1. After your think-aloud or even throughout the lesson, ask your students to reflect on strategy use. Ask them, How did I use each reciprocal teaching strategy to help me read this text, and which strategy was the most helpful?

2. Guide the use of one strategy with partners or table groups. Rather than expecting your students to produce all four strategies at once, model a think-aloud for one of the strategies, then use the following guided practice steps:

   - Guide the class in coming up with an example of the chosen strategy (for example, if you modeled a prediction, have your students help you generate another one).

   - Allow time for your students to try generating examples of the strategy by working in pairs or table groups (see Figure 11). Then, have them share with the entire class. This kind of small-group interaction encourages all students to try the strategies in a supportive environment.

Figure 11
Two Fifth-Grade Students Using the Be the Teacher Bookmark

3. Use partner practice. Have student pairs work together through a text to try the strategies aloud. Use the following scenarios:

- One student reads the text aloud and tries all four strategies.
- One student reads the text aloud, and the listening partner tries all four strategies.
- The partners alternate reading aloud and help each other with all four strategies.
- The partners alternate reading aloud, and each student chooses two reciprocal teaching strategies to try.

Assessment Tips

The following tips may help you assess your students when using the Be the Teacher Bookmark to scaffold and practice reciprocal teaching strategies:

- Circulate around the classroom and listen to your students' discussions. Are they referring to the Be the Teacher Bookmark's prompts as they work their way through the text?
- Note with which strategies your students are most and least proficient.
- Note whether your students' predictions are supported by clues from the text.
- When they are summarizing, note whether your students are just restating the text or are giving a concise summary.
- Note whether your students ask only literal questions and whether the questions are from the text.
- Note whether your students recognize several techniques for clarifying unknown words.
- Provide additional support for students struggling with the strategies by using the Be the Teacher Bookmark while meeting with small, guided reading groups.
- Use the minilessons on pages 67–71 to reinforce each individual strategy. Teach these lessons in small groups or to the entire class. Use Figure 4 (page 21) for further suggestions about what to do when your students have problems using the strategies.

Be the Teacher Bookmark

 Predict

Use clues from the text or illustrations to predict what will happen next.

I think...because...
I'll bet...because...
I suppose...because...
I think I will learn...because...

 **Question**

Ask questions as you read.
Ask some questions that have answers in the text.
Use the question words *who*, *what*, *where*, *when*, *why*, *how*, and *what if*.
Try asking some questions that can be inferred. Use clues from the text plus your experiences.

Clarify

How can you figure out a difficult word or idea in the text?

Reread, reread, reread!
Think about word chunks you know.
Try sounding it out.
Read on.
Ask, Does it make sense?
Talk to a friend.

Summarize

Using your *own* words, tell the main ideas from the text in order.

This text is about...
This part is about...

Be the Teacher Bookmark

 **Predict**

Use clues from the text or illustrations to predict what will happen next.

I think...because...
I'll bet...because...
I suppose...because...
I think I will learn...because...

Question

Ask questions as you read.
Ask some questions that have answers in the text.
Use the question words *who*, *what*, *where*, *when*, *why*, *how*, and *what if*.
Try asking some questions that can be inferred. Use clues from the text plus your experiences.

 **Clarify**

How can you figure out a difficult word or idea in the text?

Reread, reread, reread!
Think about word chunks you know.
Try sounding it out.
Read on.
Ask, Does it make sense?
Talk to a friend.

Summarize

Using your own words, tell the main ideas from the text in order.

This text is about...
This part is about...

Lesson 3: Using Cooperative Table Groups

 Predict   **Question**   **Clarify**   **Summarize**

Background and Description

In the classes with which I work, I introduce reciprocal teaching over several weeks, using texts that are very interesting and engaging for the students. After I model think-alouds using the Fabulous Four characters, use other guided lessons involving partners, and implement the Be the Teacher Bookmark, the students are ready for cooperative table groups. Having the students practice reciprocal teaching strategies before moving to cooperative table groups leads to success.

Cooperative table groups allow students to work together in small groups on a single reciprocal teaching strategy and then share their information with the entire class for an orchestrated use of all the strategies. The groups puzzle their way through the text and become experts on their assigned strategy. All the groups fill in Reciprocal Teaching Puzzles for Cooperative Table Groups (see form on page 57) to complete the meaning-making process.

The following benefits stem from using cooperative table groups:

- cooperative learning propels reciprocal teaching discussion and reading comprehension to new levels
- all four reciprocal teaching strategies are modeled and employed
- guided practice on a focus strategy at each table strengthens student expertise in the reciprocal teaching strategies

Continue referring to the general list of strategies used by good readers and the role of reciprocal teaching. Also, build your students' background knowledge regarding the text selection: For fiction, you can discuss experiences that your students might have had that relate to the text, and, for nonfiction, you can bring in photos or objects that deal with the subject matter.

- A copy of the reading material for each student in the class
- Reciprocal Teaching Puzzles for Cooperative Table Groups (page 57) to fit together all the reciprocal teaching strategies (as an option, use the form on an overhead projector)
- A Be the Teacher Bookmark (page 53) for each student

Teacher Modeling

1. Tell your students the lesson objective. Continue modeling reciprocal teaching strategies, so your students will have the opportunity to focus on one of the strategies in cooperative table groups.

2. Model reciprocal teaching strategies for your students after reading aloud a portion of the chosen text. Use either the Be the Teacher Bookmark (page 53) or the Reciprocal Teaching Puzzles for Cooperative Table Groups (page 57) to guide your think-aloud.

   Alternate modeling each strategy yourself with having table groups work on the strategies together.

Student Participation

1. Have each table group focus on one assigned strategy after you read a portion of text with the class. Have the groups share their responses with the whole class.

2. Give each group a reciprocal teaching puzzle piece and ask the group members to use the directions on the puzzle piece to lead them through their assigned strategies.

   After the groups work on their puzzle pieces, they can share with the whole class, and every four cooperative table groups can make a completed reciprocal teaching puzzle either on a poster or an overhead transparency.

   With the class, reflect on how all four strategies work together to help readers comprehend a text.

3. Have each group tell the whole class how the reciprocal teaching strategy helped group members to better understand the text.

- Circulate around the classroom and listen to the responses of the cooperative groups as they work. Are students referring to the puzzle page guidelines to help them use the reciprocal teaching strategies effectively?

- Have the table groups write their responses, and use the written responses for student assessment.

- Use your observations from this lesson to help you focus on the next steps in reciprocal teaching. See the rubric in Appendix A on page 195 for assessment guidelines for each of the four strategies. Are any strategies giving students difficulty? Do you need to model them again or use a minilesson (pages 67–71) on a single strategy to focus your students' attention? Refer to Figure 4 (page 21) for further suggestions when your students have problems using the strategies.

Reciprocal Teaching Puzzles
for Cooperative Table Groups

Predict

Predict with your group before reading. Please check off the following tasks when you have done them:

___ Preview the book's front and back cover. Discuss what you think the book is about.

___ Look through the book's illustrations and discuss them. Now, what do you think the book is about?

___ Use clues from the text or illustrations, plus your own knowledge to make a prediction or two.

___ Be prepared to explain why you made that prediction.

Discussion Points

Our predictions are

_____
_____

The prediction clues we used are

_____
_____

Question

Think about questions that you can ask others as you read the text. After reading, create some questions. Please check off the following tasks when you have done them:

___ Reread the text, looking for parts of the text that could be turned into questions.

___ Ask questions that begin with *who, what, where, when, why, how,* or *what if.*

   ___ Ask one main idea question.

   ___ Make sure you can show where your answers are in the reading.

   ___ Ask one inferential question. Explain how you used clues from the text, plus your experiences to form the question and answer.

Discussion Points

Our questions are

_____
_____
_____
_____

Reciprocal Teaching Puzzles
for Cooperative Table Groups

Clarify

Think about confusing parts or difficult words as you read. Please check off the following tasks when you have done them:

___ Reread the text, looking for difficult words or parts of the text that you did not understand.

___ Tell at least two ways to clarify difficult ideas. Reread. Read on. Think about what you know. Talk with a friend.

___ Reread the text and give one or two difficult words.

___ Explain how you figured out the difficult words. What are two strategies to use in figuring out words?

___ Reread. Think about chunks you know. Try sounding it out. Read on. Does your word make sense?

Discussion Points

A difficult word (idea) that we found is

_____

Here are the ways we figured the word (idea) out:

_____

Summarize

Summarize with your group before reading. Please check off the following tasks when you have done them:

___ Look quickly through the reading and illustrations for the main ideas. Reread, or skim and scan by running a finger and your eyes down the text to review it.

___ Use your own words to summarize the reading.

___ Make sure you summarize important events or information in order.

___ Use words such as *first, next, then,* or *finally*. For fiction, use story words such as *setting, characters, problem, key events,* and *ending*.

Discussion Points

Our summary

_____

_____

_____

_____

Lesson 4: Using Different Types of Reading Materials

Predict

Question

Clarify

Summarize

During staff development workshops, teachers often ask me what type of reading material works best for reciprocal teaching lessons. The answer is straightforward: Any and all reading material is suitable for reciprocal teaching. The strategies work naturally and are easily employed with any type of fiction or nonfiction text of any length. You can use everything from Big Books to novels to your class's social studies text, and reciprocal teaching will continue to enhance your students' reading comprehension, so you do not need to purchase any special materials for the lessons. (See the Classroom Story on page 64 for an example of this lesson taught with a newspaper article.)

Although reciprocal teaching can accelerate the reading level of students (Cooper et al., 1999), grade-level texts are preferable in reciprocal teaching lessons because students can be taught to cope with the demands of those texts in a scaffolded or supported manner. You might use easy-to-read, high-interest material that is below grade level when introducing your students to reciprocal teaching strategies, then move quickly into grade-level reading choices. During guided reading, you can apply reciprocal teaching with leveled texts that fit the reading level of the students and increase in difficulty over time. Remember that the ultimate goal of reciprocal teaching is to give students the tools to build reading comprehension skills for challenging texts.

To make reciprocal teaching work with any given text, use the strategies with workable text chunks. When introducing reciprocal teaching to a class, use paragraphs or pages as stopping points where you and your students employ reciprocal teaching strategies. You also can use lessons in textbooks, chapters in fiction books, and entire short articles as appropriate text chunks for instruction. It is easier to scaffold and support students in reciprocal teaching strategies when the text chunks are small enough for them to absorb.

This lesson outlines classroom scenarios in which teachers use reciprocal teaching to teach from different text types. It also shares how modeling and student participation may look when you are working with each of the text types. In this lesson, your students will

- use all four reciprocal teaching strategies;
- see that the reciprocal teaching strategies work with any text of any length to help them comprehend what they read; and
- begin to use the four strategies with text chunks to make comprehending longer texts more manageable.

Ask your students to reflect on the broader list of reading comprehension strategies such as previewing, making connections, and visualizing (Keene & Zimmermann, 1997; McLaughlin & Allen, 2002; Pearson et al., 1992).

See Figure 12 on page 61 for materials, teacher modeling, and student participation information.

Assessment Tips

Assess your students' use of reciprocal teaching strategies with a variety of reading materials so you can monitor and adjust your lessons to fit students' needs.

- Listen to student pairs and cooperative table groups for their reciprocal teaching responses. Collect their written responses for assessment.
- Are your students' predictions based on clues from the text or its illustrations?
- Are your students' questions literal or inferential, and are they based on the text?
- Are your students able to identify troublesome words and at least two strategies for deciphering them? Are any students identifying difficult ideas and ways to clarify them?
- Are your students' summaries succinct, including only the important points in the proper order? Do your students use language from the text in their summaries? Are their summaries getting at the text's major themes?

Figure 13 on page 63 outlines assessment tips for use with various reading materials and the whole class. These guidelines will help you determine the strategies with which students need reinforcement. Refer

Figure 12
Using Reciprocal Teaching With a Variety of Reading Materials

Reading Material	Considerations and Comments	Reciprocal Teaching Tips	Teacher Modeling	Student Participation
Big Books (fiction or nonfiction)	• These books ensure that all students can see the text. • These books make modeling explicit. • These books engage readers.	• Use page-by-page stopping points over several days. • Use more advanced nonfiction Big Books with intermediate students to model reciprocal teaching strategies.	• Model reciprocal teaching strategies page by page. • Invite students to join in the strategy use.	• Have students come up to the text and take turns with reciprocal teaching strategies. • Have partners sit in front of the text, and monitor pairs' responses.
Social Studies Textbooks	• These texts are available. • These texts are difficult for some students because of challenging concepts and vocabulary.	• Use natural breaks between lessons or sections between headings for reciprocal teaching strategies.	• Occasionally make and use overhead transparencies of pages. • Model strategies with one or more segments of text. • Point out text features—such as headings, captions, table of contents—and explain how to use them with reciprocal teaching to aid reading comprehension.	• Have tables or cooperative groups take on one of the strategies for a portion of text. • Have pairs discuss their reading with the Be the Teacher Bookmark (page 53). • Send the textbook home so parents and students can review chapters using reciprocal teaching strategies.
Reading Books (grade level anthologies and/or leveled texts)	• These books have illustrations to examine. • Anthologies are available. • Leveled texts are short. • These books offer a variety of fiction and nonfiction.	• Read the entire leveled text if it is very short, then discuss reciprocal teaching strategies.	• Model strategies during whole-class lessons or during guided reading. • Keep a chart of strategies and how you used reciprocal teaching during various selections.	• Have students work their way through the strategies in cooperative groups. • Have pairs and individuals write very briefly about each strategy (see Literature Discussion Sheet for Reciprocal Teaching on page 141).

(continued)

Figure 12 (continued)
Using Reciprocal Teaching With a Variety of Reading Materials

Reading Material	Considerations and Comments	Reciprocal Teaching Tips	Teacher Modeling	Student Participation
High-Interest Articles (in standard newspapers, magazines, or weekly classroom newspapers [*Time for Kids* or *Weekly Reader*])	• These texts are available. • These texts can be duplicated for students. • These texts can be supplied by students. • These texts are great for quick reciprocal teaching reinforcement or introductory lessons.	• You can use articles easily for reciprocal teaching because of their brevity and text features. • You can send items home or assign for reading and practicing the four strategies as homework.	• Choose one article to model strategies. • Highlight text features in reciprocal teaching strategy use, and demonstrate how those features helped you comprehend what you read.	• Ask pairs to work paragraph by paragraph on each strategy after you model it. • Have pairs continue working on their own using reciprocal teaching strategies with a designated chunk of text (a sentence, paragraph, or page).
Chapter Books (fiction novels or nonfiction texts)	• These books may be for small groups only if there are not enough copies for the entire class or even for pairs to share. • These books may not have any illustrations or other supports for predicting.	• You can use books in chunks by chapter, then have reciprocal teaching discussions.	• Make a copy of one or two pages of text to model reciprocal teaching strategies. • Model skimming and scanning when illustrations are not present; quickly run your finger down the page and call out words that catch your attention.	• You can form table groups and have tables become experts who are in charge of one reciprocal teaching strategy each. • Students can get into small groups to discuss reciprocal teaching strategies after each chapter.

Reciprocal Teaching at Work: Strategies for Improving Reading Comprehension by Lori D. Oczkus © 2003. Newark, DE: International Reading Association. May be copied for classroom use.

Figure 13
Special Assessment Tips for Various Reading Materials

Reading Material	Assessment Tips
Big Books	• Use multiple copies of the Big Book when possible, or allow your students to sit where they all can see the book. • Require every student to respond by using a whiteboard or partner activity. • Observe your students using the strategies and make adjustments to future lessons. Select one strategy as the focus for another lesson or reteach a strategy that students need to practice.
Social Studies Textbooks	• Have students work in pairs with the Be the Teacher Bookmark (page 53) to guide their responses. • Ask, Can my students identify difficult ideas and concepts, not just troublesome words? Do they know how to clarify ideas? • Have students in grades 3–6 write a brief prediction, question, clarification, or summary for discussion and sharing. Collect the writing assignment and evaluate it using the rubric in Appendix A on page 195. Meet with a small group of students who need guidance, and teach the minilessons on pages 67–71.
Reading Books (grade-level anthologies and/or leveled texts)	• Work with small groups during guided reading to assess students' use of reciprocal teaching strategies. • Have students write on self-stick notes a response for each strategy, and put the notes on a chart with their initials. • Evaluate students' use of the strategies by reading their responses and looking for incorrect or incomplete ones. • Determine which strategies students need to practice. • Teach the minilessons on pages 67–71 and continue to model the use of all four strategies. Try stopping to use the strategies after every page or paragraph for more practice. Gradually increase the text chunks as your students become more proficient with the strategies.
High-Interest Articles (in standard newspapers, magazines, or weekly classroom newspapers [*Time for Kids* or *Weekly Reader*])	• Have your students write reciprocal teaching responses directly in the margins of their reading material. Collect the responses, and evaluate them. • Provide additional modeling with another article.
Chapter Books (fiction novels and nonfiction texts)	• Have your students write a brief response for each reciprocal teaching strategy after each chapter to share with the class. • If your students have trouble, use reciprocal teaching strategies more often, maybe every few pages. Model by using a think-aloud after reading two pages of text. Invite students to participate for the next two pages of text as you work through the four strategies.

to the rubric in Appendix A on page 195 to evaluate your students' progress in reciprocal teaching. When necessary, use the minilessons at the end of the chapter to separately reinforce each reciprocal teaching strategy.

Your students can keep track of their own progress by using the self-assessment tool found in Appendix B on page 201. Remember that reciprocal teaching is a discussion technique that should not turn into a written assignment that students dread, although it is useful to have occasional written records of students' responses to the four strategies. Many forms in this book are designed to provide you with informal assessments without bogging your students down with writing. The same forms can be used to show your students' growth if you use them again with another piece of literature at a later date. If you do have your students write, make the assignment something that they will share in an oral discussion or write as a record of the discussion.

Introducing Reciprocal Teaching to Grade 6 With a Newspaper Article

It is 8:00 a.m., and I am faced with a classroom full of sleepy sixth graders who have had some formal instruction in reading strategies. I begin with the question, "What do good readers do when they read?" Knowing better than to expect immediate answers from these groggy youths, I ask them each to turn to a partner with a response first, then I encourage a whole-class discussion. Their responses include the following:

"Good readers question."

"Good readers pronounce each word correctly."

"The main idea is important."

"Sounding out words helps when you are stuck."

I assure them that good readers do all these things and more. Then, I tell them that we are going to focus on four very important strategies that good readers use to help them understand what they read.

I know I need to hook the students quickly, so I ask who likes to play basketball. Many hands go up. I tell them, "Today we are going to read a newspaper article about a young woman who loves to play basketball just like some of you, but she is paralyzed and in a wheelchair. She hasn't always been in a wheelchair. She became paralyzed at age 9 when she was just a bit younger than you. The article is about her journey to the United States Paralympic Basketball Team." I pass out copies of the article and put my copy on the overhead projector. I tell the students not to read yet because I want to model the reading strategies for them.

Predicting   "First, I am going to model predicting for you," I explain. "The first thing I am going to do is predict by reading the article's title and captions. The title reads, 'Hoops Are Haven for Orinda Paralympian' (Kilduff, 2000). I'm not sure exactly what they mean by *haven*, but I think it means that she likes basketball. The subheading says *Howitt earns spot* *on U.S. basketball team.* I predict that I will learn from the article how she got on the Paralympic Team. I should read the picture caption, too, which tells me that she is shooting for Sydney, Australia, as a point guard. The picture features her shooting a basketball from her wheelchair. I can't help but wonder how difficult it must be playing basketball from a wheelchair."

I write on the board the word *predict* and tell the students that I just previewed the article to use clues from the text to make the first of many predictions that I will formulate throughout the reading.

Questioning   After modeling prediction, I read aloud the first two paragraphs of the article, stop again, and model what I am thinking. I continue, "This article suggests that Jennifer Howitt had a tough time adjusting to being in a wheelchair. Good readers ask questions as they read, so I am wondering how she became paralyzed. If I were to ask some questions about these first paragraphs, I might ask questions that can be directly answered in the text such as, Where will the Paralympics be held this October? Who is the youngest member of the team?"

In future lessons, I will introduce the students to deeper inferential questioning. However, for now, I want them to focus on asking questions that can be answered directly in the text. They will benefit from formulating questions as they read.

Clarifying   Next, I model how to clarify a word while reading. "I had trouble reading the word *paralympic*, so I broke it down into syllables and chunks that I know. First, I read *para* and then *alympic*. I know that *para* in this word is like the chunk *para* in *paralyzed*, so that part of the word must have something to do with being disabled. *Alympic* looks like *olympic*, and I know about the Olympics as a competition. The word *paralympic* must mean a competition for disabled people. Finally, I reread the sentence to see if my word makes sense, and it does," I explain.

Summarizing   I tell the class that I am going to attempt a summary of the two paragraphs that I just read. One of my favorite summarizing techniques to model is rereading, so I tell them that I usually need to reread the portion of text that I am about to summarize at least twice. After doing that, I announce that I am ready to take a stab at summarizing. I state, "Jennifer Howitt has adjusted to life in a wheelchair by competing in wheelchair basketball. She is the youngest woman on the U.S. Paralympic Basketball team, and she will compete in Australia in October."

Predicting Again   So the students can see how to predict what the next portion of text holds, I model how to predict when engaged in the middle of an article. I continue, "I am going to glance at the first sentence of the next paragraph before I predict, and I will combine those clues with what I already know about the article to formulate a new prediction for the next portion of text. The next sentence tells about how Jennifer was injured, so I predict that the next portion of text will tell how she became paralyzed and how she felt about it at first. It might even tell about her interest in wheelchair sports."

Cooperative Table Groups and Partners: An Intermediate Scaffolded Step

To further scaffold the learning experience, I work with the entire class for another three paragraphs and then use cooperative table groups in which six students have their desks grouped together. Using the article on the overhead projector, I read two paragraphs aloud and stop to ask each table group to work together and come up with a question that is answered in the text. The students huddle together to reread the paragraphs, and each group eagerly discusses ideas. When I signal the class to focus up front, I begin calling on each group to respond. When I ask for a question, Juan replies, "How was Jennifer Howitt injured?" I encourage Juan to call on students from other groups to answer his question. We continue with each table group asking questions, and then I ask each group to generate a summary, a word to clarify, and a prediction for the next portion of text.

Next, I ask each student to work with a partner and read two paragraphs at a time, using the four strategies as they read and discuss. Each partner takes a turn reading, and the other partner uses all four strategies in a think-aloud. I encourage the students to use the Be the Teacher Bookmark to guide their discussions. I circulate around the room to monitor the activity and offer further guidance to pairs who need it.

I listen in on Ali and Isa as they work their way through the four strategies. Ali says, "I need to clarify the word *traumatized*. I knew the word *trauma* and then sounded the rest out, but I still don't know what it means." "I think if you reread the paragraph, it helps," claims Isa. "*Traumatized* means that when the guy flipped her out of her wheelchair, she felt horrible, sad," she says. I decide to interject an example of how to clarify an idea because many students need more modeling before they are adept at verbalizing their confusions. "I think it is hard to understand why the team member flipped her out of her chair. I needed to clarify that myself. I reread and am going to infer that he did it for fun and not to be mean because when I have watched wheelchair basketball, I have seen the players do things like that to tease each other." Ali and Isa indicate that they now understand that part of the text, and I move on.

After listening to several students, I hear many of them asking questions about how the teams for wheelchair basketball are organized and played. I decide that, in addition to reviewing all four strategies when I pull the class together to wrap up the lesson, I also will mention that many of them needed to clarify ideas on the topic. I am grateful for the natural invitation to model and guide them to use clarifying beyond the word level.

Reflection and Next Steps After the students finish the article, I ask the class to discuss the four reciprocal teaching strategies and how those strategies work together to help them read:

Eduardo: These strategies made me think about what I was reading.

Samantha: Questioning is fun.

Mrs. Oczkus: Tell what was fun about questioning.

Samantha: Because we get to ask other kids questions.

Trevor: Summarizing was tough.

Mrs. Oczkus: What was so hard about summarizing? Please give us a detail.

Trevor: It is hard to make the paragraphs shorter. We had to reread every time.

In future weeks, the classroom teacher and I will continue to model reciprocal teaching with newspaper articles. Then, we will use reciprocal teaching with the class's social studies text while the students continue working cooperatively in table groups and pairs.

Minilesson: What's Your Prediction?

Description and Comprehension Strategies

Have students make predictions in groups and share them with others in stroll lines—two lines of students situated across from each other. Comprehension strategies include using textual clues to make logical predictions.

Materials

multiple copies of a text with illustrations

Teacher Modeling

1. Ask your students how good readers make predictions. Chart their responses.

2. Model for your students how to use clues from the text and illustration to make predictions.

Student Participation

1. Assign pages of the text to cooperative groups, and have the groups meet to write predictions for their pages. Each group member will need a copy of the predictions to share during the stroll-line activity.

2. Have the class form two lines that face one another. Instruct the students who are across from one another to work as pairs and share their predictions and clues with each other.

    Then, signal all the students in one of the lines to move one person to the right and the student at the end to move to the front of the line. Have the new partners share their predictions.

    Continue switching partners and sharing until each student has shared with at least three others.

3. Debrief the prediction-sharing experience as a whole class. List some of the predictions on a piece of butcher paper or a whiteboard. Have students begin reading the text, and use the list to check predictions after reading.

Assessment Tip

Are your students using text and illustration clues to make logical predictions? Model predicting for and guide small groups of students who are having difficulty providing evidence for their predictions.

Minilesson: Pick a Question

Description and Comprehension Strategies

Students work in pairs, then as a whole class to ask questions after reading a text. Comprehension strategies include using a variety of question words to formulate questions.

Materials

multiple copies of the text and paper strips with the question words *who*, *what*, *when*, *where*, *why*, *how*, and *what if*

Teacher Modeling

Model the steps for asking a variety of questions that begin with *who*, *what*, *where*, *when*, *why*, *how*, and *what if*, using a meaningful portion of text, such as a chapter.

Student Participation

1. Make cards or paper strips with each of the question words. Mix them up, then turn them over or put them in a hat so students can choose them one at a time.

2. Read the question word, and ask student pairs to work together to create a question based on the text that begins with the selected word.

3. Encourage the student pairs to share their questions and answers first with one another and then with the class.

4. Ask your students to reflect on and share ideas for creating good questions.

Assessment Tips

Can your students use the question words to write their own text questions? Can they ask main idea and inferential questions or only questions about details? Model questioning in small groups for students who need reinforcement, or put students in literature circles (see chapter 4) to draw question-word strips from the hat and use them to discuss a book or article that the class has already read together.

Minilesson: Clarifying With the *Independent Strategies* Poem

Description and Comprehension Strategies

Use the following poem in a series of lessons to help students identify words that need to be clarified and a plan for deciphering the words. The comprehension strategy is how to clarify words as students reread the poem.

Independent Strategies by Jill Marie Warner
(Reprinted from *The Reading Teacher*, 48(6), p. 710. Copyright 1996 by the
   International Reading Association.)

When I get stuck on a word in a book,
There are lots of things to do.
I can do them all, please, by myself;
I don't need help from you.

I can look at the picture to get a hint,
Or think what the story's about.
I can "get my mouth ready" to say the first letter,
A kind of "sounding out."
I can chop the word into smaller parts,
Like *on* and *ing* and *by*,
Or find smaller words in compound words
Like *raincoat* and *bumblebee*.
I can think of a word that makes sense in that place,
Guess or say "blank" and read on:
   "Does it make sense?"
   "Can we say it that way?"
   "Does it *look* right to me?"
Chances are the right word will pop out like the sun
In my *own* mind, can't you see?

If I've thought of and tried out most of these things
And I *still* do not know what to do,
Then I may turn around and ask
For some help to get me through.

(continued)

Materials
multiple copies of the poem and a chart, whiteboard, or overhead projector

Teacher Modeling
1. Ask your students what good readers do when they come to a word that they do not know. Chart their responses and display them in the classroom.

2. Read the poem aloud, and invite your students to join in. Return to the response chart, and ask your students to add to their original ideas for clarifying words.

3. Choose a few strategies to model each day with any reading material.

Student Participation
1. Vary the ways to read and share the poem, such as having two groups alternate reading lines or having tables read lines in rotation. Use the cloze procedure by leaving out words for your students to supply.

2. Encourage your students to use these strategies with peers.

Assessment Tip
Are your students using a variety of clarifying strategies from the poem? Choose one of the poem's strategies each day to model in material that the class is reading. Send the poem home for parents to read and use with their children to reinforce the reciprocal teaching strategies.

Minilesson: Table Group Summaries

Description and Comprehension Strategies

Students work first in cooperative groups and then as a class to construct a summary of a text. Comprehension strategies include summarizing with ideas in proper order and selecting main ideas.

Materials

multiple copies of the text; paper strips or sheets, overhead transparencies, or a large or pocket chart; and an overhead projector if using transparencies

Teacher Modeling

Model the steps for telling a summary with the main events or important facts in the order that they appear within the text. Use a meaningful portion of text, such as a chapter.

Student Participation

1. Break the summary into parts—the beginning, middle, and end. Assign or let cooperative groups choose which portion of the text they will summarize and draw.

2. Have all the groups share their portion of the summary verbally or in writing. As the tables share their information in order, they can bring their summary piece to a whiteboard, large or pocket chart, or overhead transparency at the front of the classroom to construct the group retelling. Drawings are optional.

3. Have the class reread the group summary.

Assessment Tips

- After the group summary, can your students reconstruct their own summaries of the text? Monitor them to see if they tell key events or facts in order. If any of them are having difficulty, model summarizing with a small group or write a class summary together. Eventually, ask groups to write summaries, and share them with the class. Then, have the class vote on the summary they think is the best.
- Create a class rubric about what makes a good summary by analyzing summaries the class and groups have written.

CHAPTER SUMMARY

- Whole-class instruction with reciprocal teaching offers students a sense of community and the opportunity to develop a common language about reciprocal teaching.

- Whole-class instruction needs to be sprinkled with ways to engage and actively involve all students. By weaving in the Be the Teacher Bookmark (page 53) and periodic partner and cooperative group activities, whole-class sessions can become engaging and memorable for students.

- The goals of whole-class instruction include establishing a common language for using reciprocal teaching strategies, increasing opportunities for scaffolding the strategies, and providing time to practice the strategies before students move into literature circles.

- It may be necessary to gather the whole class for a variety of purposes, including introducing and modeling the reciprocal teaching strategies, but then you might return to a small-group setting to ensure that students are understanding the strategies.

- Four foundations must be in place to maximize the effectiveness of reciprocal teaching: scaffolding, think-alouds, metacognition, and cooperative learning.

- You can use the whole-class setting to introduce students to reciprocal teaching. Try using props such as the Be the Teacher Bookmark and the Fabulous Four characters to help your students remember the strategies. Model the strategies as a package rather than individually.

- To assess students during whole-class instruction, observe pairs and groups at work. Watch for proper strategy use, and occasionally have students write their responses to the strategies.

- You can use any available reading materials with reciprocal teaching, such as Big Books, textbooks, leveled texts, high-interest newspaper or magazine articles, and chapter books.

Reflections for Group Study, Self-Study, or Staff Development

1 What are the goals of whole-class sessions using reciprocal teaching strategies?

2 Tell how you might introduce the four reciprocal teaching strategies with a reading selection, reinforce a strategy that students are having trouble with, or model procedures for literature circles.

3 How can you avoid having only a few students or the same students raise their hands during whole-class sessions?

4 What are some ways of enhancing the sense of community during whole-class reciprocal teaching sessions?

5 How can you use cooperative learning during whole-class sessions to scaffold reciprocal teaching instruction?

6 Give some models for moving from whole-class to small-group instruction. Also, tell when and how you might first instruct students in the strategies in small groups and then move to a whole-class setting.

7 What are the roles of scaffolding, think-alouds, metacognition, and cooperative learning during whole-class reciprocal teaching sessions?

8 How can you effectively assess students' use of reciprocal teaching strategies during whole-class sessions?

9 How will you reinforce reciprocal teaching throughout the school year in whole-class sessions?

10 Try this chapter's lessons and reflect on how your students did with the strategies. Circulate around the room during partner and cooperative group interactions, and record your students' responses to share with colleagues. What will you do next to deepen your students' understanding and use of reciprocal teaching strategies?

CHAPTER 3

RECIPROCAL TEACHING

in Guided Reading Groups

Clarify helps me understand words I don't know. So, the next time I
see the word I'll know what it means.

—*Francisco, grade 4*

Description of Reciprocal Teaching and Guided Reading

Guided reading—small-group instruction that is teacher led and teacher directed—often has been referred to as the heart of a reading program (Fountas & Pinnell, 1996). In this setting, students are organized into flexible groups that change based on regular assessments. As the name *guided reading* indicates, the teacher guides students through a text, which may be at a slightly more difficult level than the students could read on their own. Returning to the bicycle-riding metaphor, it is helpful to compare guided reading to holding on to the back of a child's bicycle seat while he or she pedals because the scaffolding that teachers give students during guided reading requires varying degrees of "holding on to the bicycle seat" or "running alongside" students to lend them support. Guided reading offers opportunities for rich scaffolding that may include teacher modeling of or coaching in the reciprocal teaching strategies, or student interaction with peers in a variety of lessons.

Many primary teachers today employ a strategic type of guided reading that uses meaningful text and good reader strategies such as making predictions and using various strategies to figure out unknown words. Many of these strategies are borrowed from intervention programs for struggling primary students (Clay, 1985, 1993; Hiebert & Taylor, 1994; Pikulski, 1994), and they include

- rereading a familiar text to build fluency and comprehension,
- previewing illustrations and text prior to reading,
- making predictions,
- reading silently,
- coaching students in strategies for figuring out unknown words, and
- participating in word work (manipulating letters, sounds, word parts, and/or syllables using manipulatives, writing activities, and games).

In addition to the powerful teaching strategies found in early interventions, educators also have learned from the interventions how to (a) assess students by listening to their oral reading, (b) use more natural-sounding leveled texts (texts that were leveled according to difficulty and certain criteria [Peterson, 1991]), and (c) match students' reading abilities to leveled texts (Fountas & Pinnell, 1996).

The unique literacy needs of intermediate and middle school students may include struggles with decoding, comprehension, or fluency. A group of teacher researchers (Cooper et al., 2000) searching for effective and appropriate strategies to use in a small-group intervention model for intermediate students decided to use reciprocal teaching. They knew that if used consistently, reciprocal teaching could yield dramatic positive results, so they designed an intervention model based on what educators know about effective intervention for intermediate students (Cooper et al., 1999), which includes the successful use of graphic organizers.

Cooper and colleagues (2000) successfully field-tested the following reading strategies in their small-group model:

- *Revisiting* familiar texts for fluency and comprehension (Samuels, 1979)

- *Reviewing* selected content using graphic organizers

- *Rehearsing*, or previewing, the text using the illustrations and headings, introducing a graphic organizer, and setting purposes for reading

- *Reading* and then using *reciprocal teaching* strategies to discuss the text

- *Responding to* and *reflecting on* one's own thoughts and feelings on the reading selection and self-evaluating one's performance as a reader (Sweet, 1993)

After using what Cooper and colleagues (2000) named the Project Success Model for 76 days of instruction, the researchers found that the students in the research group performed significantly better than the control group on measures of retelling, question answering, and reading comprehension. Also, higher percentages of students in the control group were able to read on grade level after a subsequent period of instruction with the Project Success Model. These promising results make reciprocal teaching an attractive technique worth considering for enhancing your students' reading comprehension skills.

I began using reciprocal teaching in my guided reading groups about seven years ago and am constantly amazed at the results. Prior to using reciprocal teaching, I was already using predicting, questioning, clarifying, and summarizing with students during small-group instruction. However, when I formally introduced reciprocal teaching strategies to students and scaffolded the instruction to include reflection on strategy use, I witnessed their improvement in reading comprehension.

I have used reciprocal teaching with both primary and intermediate students. As I reflect on my past experiences with guided reading, it helps me to understand the impact of reciprocal teaching. The type of small-group, guided reading instruction that I lead with students now looks very different from the ability-grouping juggling act that I performed when I first started teaching over 20 years ago. At that time, teachers used unnatural-sounding basal readers, placed students in stagnant groups based on ability, and asked students to take turns reading aloud. Because I was a bilingual teacher, I had the additional challenge of teaching at least one or two groups in Spanish. I also had to come up with loads of seatwork to keep students busy while I met with each group. I can remember waking up in the night in a guilty panic and thinking, "Oh, no, I didn't meet with the Cookie Monsters group today!" I meant well, but the practices that today's educators know are effective for organizing and instructing teacher-led groups are so much more effective in helping students to become better readers.

This chapter contains many creative options for incorporating guided reading groups and reciprocal teaching strategies. All the lessons engage students with the text, the teacher, and one another and include strategies to use before, during, and after reading. (See Figure 14 for an overview of the lessons presented in this chapter.) The lessons also address the following instructional elements: background building or discussion of students' prior knowledge, a picture or text preview during which your students form predictions and ask questions, a silent-reading period in which you move around the room and coach individual students in reciprocal teaching strategies, and a discussion of the text during which you might use a graphic organizer or another reciprocal teaching discussion format.

Throughout guided reading lessons, encourage your students to interact with one another by previewing the text, reading, discussing important text points, asking questions, and reflecting on strategy use together. I have discovered that a well-run guided reading group in which students are led through a reciprocal teaching discussion can serve as a training ground for eventual use of reciprocal teaching strategies during literature circles (see chapter 4).

Figure 14
Lesson Overview Chart: Reciprocal Teaching With Guided Reading Groups

Lesson	Pages	Description
A Guided Reading Plan for Fiction and Nonfiction	90 to 100	Lesson plans to use with reciprocal teaching and any fiction or nonfiction text
Using Comprehension Charts	101 to 108	Comprehension charts to use include the Basic Comprehension Chart for Guided Reading Groups, the Reciprocal Teaching Guided Reading Nonfiction Chart, the Know-Want-Learn Reciprocal Teaching Chart for Guided Reading, and the Story Map Prediction Chart
Coaching Students in Reciprocal Teaching During Guided Reading	109 to 115	Reciprocal teaching coaching prompts for guided reading groups
Using Movie or Television Clips and Freeze Frames to Retell and Summarize	116 to 120	Retellings using movie or television clips and summaries using freeze frames
Using the Clarifying Bookmarks	121 to 123	A bookmark tool for clarifying both words and ideas
Minilesson: Predicting With the Table of Contents	124	Tables of contents used to make predictions
Minilesson: Questioning With the Table of Contents	125	Table of contents used to question before and after reading
Minilesson: Creating a Group Clarify Poster	126	Creating a chart of strategies for clarifying
Minilesson: Partner Page Summary	127	Partners taking turns summarizing pages of the text

Goals of Reciprocal Teaching During Guided Reading

The goals of reciprocal teaching during guided reading instruction are

- to model the reciprocal teaching strategies and guide students to use them;
- to guide students to use effective strategies before, during, and after reading to comprehend the text;
- to allow all students to benefit from a small-group setting;
- to teach comprehension strategies for texts that the students would not be able to read and understand as easily on their own;
- to expose students to more teacher modeling of reciprocal teaching strategies;
- to group students flexibly, based on regular assessments to better meet their needs;
- to guide students through interactive lessons that prepare them for literature circles and other group discussions; and
- to help students to reflect on use of the reciprocal teaching strategies.

Many teachers already use some reciprocal teaching strategies during guided reading, but, when the four strategies are taught as a package, students have the opportunity to become even more metacognitive and flexible in using them.

Organizing Guided Reading Groups in Your Classroom

The three traditional reading groups of high-, low-, and middle-range achievers are what many teachers and parents think of when they hear the words *reading groups*; however, educators now know that it is not recommended to maintain these traditional groupings all year. Convincing research points to many reasons for flexibly grouping students instead, and the studies on the negative effects of ability grouping are worth considering when you are deciding how to group your students for literacy instruction. For example, consider that low-range achievers often suffer from low self-esteem and receive lower quality instruction (Slavin, 1987) and the self-fulfilling prophecy that "once a blue bird, always a blue bird" (referring to the name sometimes given to the low-achieving readers' group) often becomes a reality as a low achiever moves through the grades. Recent studies on intervention (Cooper et al., 1999, 2000; Pikulski, 1994) indicate that schools should provide their struggling readers three to five times per week with an additional 30–40-minute intervention lesson plan that is carefully designed to deliver high-quality strategic reading instruction. Although there are some benefits to high achievers working together (Johnson & Johnson, 1992), studies on ability grouping have found that flexible grouping combined with differentiated instruction also can lead to gains for more able students (Kulik & Kulik, 1992). Overall, when you determine the arrangement of small groups, your goal should be to change the groupings based on the students' needs and their proficiency with both the text and reciprocal teaching strategies.

You can keep the guided reading groups flexible in many ways so your students are not stuck in the same group all year. The four main ways to group and place students into reciprocal teaching groups are as follows:

1. Strategy Needs Groups: Students are placed in a group because they need work on one specific reciprocal teaching strategy. I change these groups at least twice a month and sometimes weekly, and I use minilessons on the strategy (see the minilessons in this chapter and in chapters 2 and 4). You can use any of the forms in this book (especially the Literature Discussion Sheet for Reciprocal Teaching on page 141) as assessment tools for determining which students need to focus on a given strategy.

2. Student Choice Groups: Students select their reading material based on interest, and you meet in guided reading groups with the students who have selected the same titles. In these groups, a struggling reader who chooses a more difficult book but is interested in reading it often can succeed beyond your expectations.

3. Intervention Groups for Struggling Readers: Try to organize a formal after-school, in-class, or pull-out intervention that does not replace the regular classroom instruction but is similar to an extra reading supervitamin that is administered for 30–40 minutes, three to five

times per week. Although you should begin by using literature that is slightly below grade level, once your students are proficient using all four reciprocal teaching strategies, you can accelerate the reading choices to grade-level material (Cooper et al., 1999). In addition to participating in the intervention group, the struggling students should read the core literature with the entire class, participate in mixed-ability guided reading groups, and take literature circle roles (see chapter 4 for discussion of literature circles).

You can use the intervention groups to give struggling readers the advantage. In several classrooms, I have introduced reciprocal teaching strategies to intervention students over many months during guided reading. Then, when they are proficient in the strategies, I introduce the rest of the class to reciprocal teaching strategies with the intervention students serving as the resident reciprocal teaching experts. The intervention students love their role as the authorities on reciprocal teaching.

4. Ability Groups: In first- and second-grade classrooms, I meet a few times a week with groups whose members read at the same level. Students are given an overall reading assessment that tells at what grade level they are reading for both instruction and independent reading, then they are grouped with students at similar levels. Teach reciprocal teaching strategies to the groups, using materials that fit each group's reading level. I try to minimize the use of this type of ability grouping after second grade because of the negative effects that ability grouping can have on students' self-esteem and achievement. These ability-based guided reading groups are part of a broader grouping plan in which all students participate in whole-class instruction and mixed-ability literature circles.

Figure 15 outlines the four flexible groupings and suggests ways to assess your students' placement in the appropriate groups.

Materials for Guided Reading: Thinking Beyond "Little Books"

Many teachers use leveled texts or "little books" with guided reading groups. The books often are organized in bins according to reading level or Reading Recovery level (Peterson, 1991) and are matched to students'

Figure 15
Guidelines for Placing Students Into Reciprocal Teaching Groups

Type of Group	Assessment for Placement	Suggestions
Strategy Needs	• Assess students' proficiency in each reciprocal teaching strategy using a variety of tools including observation during discussion, many of the forms in this book (for example, the Literature Discussion Sheet for Reciprocal Teaching on page 141), and the rubric in Appendix A (page 195).	• Change strategy groups often, perhaps every time the class reads a new text selection. • Have students who have difficulty using reciprocal teaching strategies in a given genre (for example, summarizing nonfiction texts) work on the classroom text or an easier text to practice the strategy.
Student Choice	• Have students choose the title that they want to read, which will become the criteria for group placement. • Have students give first and second choices of texts to read.	• Place books where students may peruse them before choosing a title. • Meet with each group regularly to lead the reciprocal teaching discussion.
Intervention for Struggling Readers	• Place students in this group based on reading level. Intervention students should be at least 1–2 years below their grade level in reading skills. • Use an overall reading assessment to measure a student's grade level of reading. The assessment should include reading passages at a variety of grade levels, in addition to comprehension items or a retelling. • Continue performing ongoing oral reading and comprehension checks with the students.	• If possible, give this group their extra 30-minute dose of reading instruction using reciprocal teaching strategies in an intervention after or before school. Otherwise, incorporate intervention group time into regular class time at least three times per week. • Introduce this group's members to reciprocal teaching first, making them the experts for literature circles.
Ability Level	• Listen to and score students' oral reading. • Also, score students' overall comprehension to find their reading levels and grade levels.	• In grades 3–6, rely more on flexible and interest groupings and less on this type of grouping. • Use leveled texts with this group.

Reciprocal Teaching at Work: Strategies for Improving Reading Comprehension by Lori D. Oczkus © 2003. Newark, DE: International Reading Association. May be copied for classroom use.

abilities according to where they place on an assessment (usually a record of a child's reading level as measured by his or her score on oral reading passages). Although these materials are incredibly valuable to guided reading, especially in grades K–3 when students are first learning to read, you should use many other rich materials during guided reading.

Some great reading material sources—especially for grades 3–6—are

- your school district's adopted reading series (ideal for reciprocal teaching practice because of the wide variety of genres and shorter reading selections);
- newspaper articles (great for minilessons on high-interest topics);
- poems (ideal for brief, practical lessons both for summarizing and analyzing word patterns when clarifying);
- magazines (short articles on high-interest topics can be used in small groups);
- picture books for nonfiction topics (work well with primary and second-language students because of opportunities for use of all four strategies on every page);
- novels (ideal for chapter-by-chapter use of reciprocal teaching strategies);
- real-world texts such as maps, menus, travel brochures, and directions for machines, for example, how to program the VCR (fun to read and offer short selections for use in guided reading groups); and
- social studies, science, and health textbooks (can be used in small-group settings to teach students how to read nonfiction texts).

Textbooks and Guided Reading

Although many text types can be used with reciprocal teaching in guided reading groups, in this section I elaborate on textbooks because many teachers struggle with how to use them to teach reading comprehension. Social studies and science textbooks are practical and available resources for guided reading groups and reciprocal teaching strategies. One day when I visited Glorianna Chen's third-grade class, the students in her guided reading group were working their way through a chapter in a science text (see Figure 16). They were busy previewing the headings and pictures, making predictions about what they thought they would learn, and reading silently. Glorianna explained to me that she was going

Figure 16
Glorianna Chen Works With Students in a Guided Reading Group

to meet with one group per day to preview and begin reading the science chapter. Her rationale for using the science text during guided reading was twofold and simple: (1) She has found it efficient to use the content area material that she needs to cover within guided reading sessions, and (2) she has found that many students pay better attention to the text in a small-group setting.

Textbooks are a ready source of material to use to practice reciprocal teaching strategies, and I like to use a lesson or a few pages in a guided reading lesson with reciprocal teaching strategies. I especially enjoy predicting with textbooks because they are loaded with illustrations, maps, charts, and other nonfiction text features that make great minilessons for educators to focus on during guided reading lessons. I call mixed-ability groups up to the reading table to preview, predict, and read silently. After reading, my students make quick summaries and ask each other questions. We choose one idea and one word that we need to clarify. Although I cannot get very far in the text with a group using this method, I can send the students back to their desks and ask them to work through the next text chunk with reciprocal teaching strategies, or I can conduct interactive whole-class lessons with the remaining portions of the text selection.

The Big Picture in Guided Reading: What Else You Will Need to Do

Although reciprocal teaching during guided reading sessions strengthens students' reading comprehension, there are other types of lesson plans that students may need to further their reading comprehension skills. Guided reading requires your understanding of all the reading comprehension strategies that students need and the classroom management techniques associated with small-group instruction. Conducting effective guided reading sessions requires that you

- assess where students are and continually assess their reading levels and strategy use,
- use effective strategies to meet students' needs,
- keep groups flexible and based on students' needs,
- create effective lesson plans for fiction and nonfiction texts,
- plan for regular times to meet with guided reading groups,
- address reading fluency through rereadings of familiar materials, and
- employ effective classroom management strategies such as centers or meaningful seatwork to keep other students busy.

Students in grades K–2 may need guided reading lessons that focus more on decoding and word-level strategies. Those guided reading lessons also may focus on word work in which students build words from the selection's vocabulary using magnetic letters or letter cards (Cunningham & Cunningham, 1992). Sometimes you may opt to lead primary students in an interactive writing lesson in which your students take turns and help the group write a message on a chart.

Students in grades 3–6 who are reading sophisticated novels may need time to have an open discussion in which they can discuss their feelings, the author's craft, character motives, opinions about the text's content, or connections that they have to the text. These lively exchanges may not fit neatly into the boundaries of reciprocal teaching strategies, yet it is valuable to take the time during guided reading lessons to discuss the emotional issues related to the reading experience.

With struggling students, you also can use guided reading groups to build background information and key vocabulary. This instruction prepares them for working in a whole-class session with a text. During guided reading groups with struggling students, reciprocal teaching is an especially effective technique (Cooper et al., 2000).

A burning issue that concerns many teachers regarding guided reading is what to do with the rest of the class while you are working with a small group. One staff developer, Susan Page, uses familiar routines and what she calls *smart work* to keep her students engaged in meaningful ways. Familiar routines are activities that students are trained in fully and participate in regularly. *Smart work* is a clever term that I have borrowed and used in several schools, and students enjoy using the term and all that it implies. The students' routines that become smart work might include reading alone or with partners, filling in graphic organizers, preparing a read-aloud for a cross-age buddy, and participating in word work with spelling words. I prefer asking students to spend much of their smart-work time reading in real texts rather than filling out worksheets that isolate reading skills.

A very creative solution to keeping students busy during guided reading groups is to allow the rest of the class to participate in literature circles (see chapter 4) while you meet with one group. It also is very helpful not to feel that you have to meet with every group every day. Doing so is nearly impossible and will probably cause you undue stress. However, you should try to meet with students in grades 2–3 at least three times a week in a guided reading setting and with students in grades 4–6 at least once a week. The exception is, of course, the struggling readers group that needs to meet three to five times a week either during class or before or after school in a special, teacher-led intervention group.

For more information on using guided reading groups in your classroom, see the book suggestions in Figure 17.

Assessment Options for Reciprocal Teaching During Guided Reading

Many excellent opportunities exist for assessing individual students' use of reciprocal teaching strategies during guided reading groups. The small-

---

Figure 17
Books on Guided Reading

Allington, R.L. (Ed.). (1998). *Teaching struggling readers: Articles from* The Reading Teacher. Newark, DE: International Reading Association.

Fountas, I.C., & Pinnell, G.S. (1996). *Guided reading: Good first teaching for all children.* Portsmouth, NH: Heinemann.

Fountas, I.C., & Pinnell, G.S. (2001). *Guiding readers and writers (grades 3–6): Teaching comprehension, genre, and content literacy.* Portsmouth, NH: Heinemann.

Opitz, M.F., & Ford, M.P. (2001). *Reaching readers: Flexible and innovative strategies for guided reading.* Portsmouth, NH: Heinemann.

Routman, R. (1999). *Conversations: Strategies for teaching, learning, and evaluating.* Portsmouth, NH: Heinemann.

Schulman, M.B., & DaCruz, C. (2000). *Guided reading: Making it work (grades K–3).* New York: Scholastic.

---

group format allows for more student participation and increased opportunities for observing them in action with the strategies and various types of texts. Refer to the reciprocal teaching rubric in Appendix A (page 195) for detailed guidelines on what to look for when observing students who are engaging in a reciprocal teaching discussion. Also, refer to Figure 4 (page 21) for ways to overcome the difficulties that students experience with reciprocal teaching strategies.

The following guidelines will help you assess reciprocal teaching during guided reading lessons:

- Observe your students during reciprocal teaching discussions. Listen closely to them as they predict, question, clarify, and summarize. Use the reciprocal teaching rubric in Appendix A (page 195) as a checklist at the guided reading table. Either focus on one student per day and note how he or she uses all the strategies, or focus on one strategy and observe all students' use of that strategy.

- Coach and assess individual students during silent reading. When your students are busy reading on their own during guided reading, take turns sitting next to each student for a quick individual coaching session. Take a few notes regarding student progress during these quick assessments so you can keep track of strategies with which each student struggles. Coaching students during guided reading lessons gives them individual attention and

Figure 18
Guided Reading Coaching Prompts

Reciprocal Teaching Strategy	Prompt(s)
Predict	Tell me what you think will happen next in the text. Why do you think that is so?
Question	What is a question that you could ask about this page? What is the answer? How did you get that answer?
Clarify	Identify a difficult word or concept. How did you figure it out? Give at least two ways.
Summarize	Summarize this paragraph, page, or chapter. Or, summarize what we have read so far.

gives you time to assess them. (See prompts to use during guided reading in Figure 18.)

• Use brief, written responses from students during guided reading lessons as informal assessments of their progress with reciprocal teaching. Assignments may include having your students write predictions, questions, summaries, or ways to clarify words or ideas on self-stick notes for the group's graphic organizer. Have your students put their names or initials on the notes so you can identify and assess each student's work. Also, have students fill out any forms in this book that apply to the strategy or strategies that you are modeling and guiding (for example, use the Literature Discussion Sheet for Reciprocal Teaching on page 141).

Lesson 1: A Guided Reading Plan for Fiction and Nonfiction

Predict

Question

Clarify

Summarize

Background and Description

Although you should vary your lessons on reciprocal teaching in guided reading depending on your students' grade level and reading selections, some consistent and effective reciprocal teaching routines are worth considering. For example, the lesson plans that I use to guide my teaching have some of the same before-, during-, and after-reading elements such as building background, predicting, thinking of questions to ask classmates during reading, asking questions after reading, clarifying points and words, and summarizing. This lesson uses reciprocal teaching with fiction and nonfiction texts and incorporates before-, during-, and after-reading tasks. In some schools where I consult, the teachers and I use this lesson plan as a guide when we coach and observe each other's use of reciprocal teaching.

There are some differences when teaching a guided reading lesson using reciprocal teaching with nonfiction instead of fiction. Predicting is slightly different with nonfiction because you can ask students what they think they will learn instead of what they think will happen next. Summarizing with fiction may center on story elements, including a problem and the main events, but summarizing with nonfiction varies depending on how the text is organized, and it requires students to select the main ideas and supporting details. Also, when teaching with nonfiction texts, it is helpful to discuss text features such as captions, diagrams, maps, and indexes during guided reading lessons.

This lesson requires the use of

- all four reciprocal teaching strategies;
- before-, during-, and after-reading applications of reciprocal teaching; and
- reflections on strategy use.

You also will need

- background knowledge building or prior knowledge activation related to topics in the text;

- time for students to freely respond to the text about their feelings, the author's craft, evaluations of character motives, and/or important or thought-provoking ideas in the text; and

- other reading comprehension strategies, such as visualization, as needed (Keene & Zimmermann, 1997; McLaughlin & Allen, 2002; Pearson et al., 1992)

Materials

- Multiple copies of the text to read with the guided reading group
- Paper to create a comprehension chart
- Copies of the Clarifying Bookmarks (see bookmarks on page 95)
- Coaching suggestions from Figure 18 on page 89

Teacher Modeling and Student Participation

Before Reading: Predict and Summarize

1. Discuss the book's title, cover illustrations, and information on the back cover. Model predictions for your students and have them make some initial predictions.

2. As an option, record your students' predictions on a comprehension chart—a concrete place for chronicling discussions, responses, and reflections. Create your own chart, or use the Basic Comprehension Chart for Guided Reading Groups (for fiction or nonfiction; see chart on page 96), Reciprocal Teaching Guided Reading Nonfiction Chart (see chart on page 97), the Know-Want-Learn Reciprocal Teaching Chart for Guided Reading (for nonfiction; see chart on page 98), or the Story Map Prediction Chart (for fiction; see chart on page 99). Use the appropriate chart throughout the lesson as necessary to monitor your students' reading comprehension and discussions.

3. If you are using fiction, discuss students' experiences that relate to the book to activate their prior knowledge. If you are using a nonfiction text, ask your students what they know about the topic of the text. Fill in the "What We Know (About)" section of the chosen chart.

4. Or, if you are in the middle of a text with a group, summarize the last reading selection before previewing the current one. Refer to the comprehension chart that you have selected to use.

5. Have your students work in pairs or as a group with you to preview illustrations in fiction texts, or headings, illustrations, captions, and maps in nonfiction texts. When there are no illustrations in either text, have your students skim and scan the chapter or pages for a minute or two. Model for them how to skim, scan, and hunt for key story words.

6. Predict again and show your students how to use clues from the preview to make predictions. Allow your students to offer predictions verbally or on self-stick notes, and remind them to monitor their predictions as they read. Ask them, What do you think you will learn? What clues did you use?

   Encourage your students to think about questions that they would like to have answered. Add their predictions and questions to the comprehension chart that you have selected for this lesson.

During Reading: Question and Clarify

1. Encourage your students to hunt for portions of text that would make good questions to ask others after reading. Provide self-stick notes for recording the questions and give an example that your students can follow.

2. Remind your students to use their copies of the Clarifying Bookmarks (page 95) to help them with words or ideas that are tricky. Ask them to be prepared to share with the class one difficult spot in the text and how they clarified it. You may wish to model this activity before asking your students to do it.

3. Have your students read the text selection silently while you rotate to individuals and coach them in the reciprocal teaching strategies. Do not use round-robin reading because it does not promote reading comprehension (see Opitz & Rasinski, 1998).

4. Encourage your students to reread the text to ask questions or identify clarifications. Self-stick notes are an optional place for students to write their questions or clarifications. They should initial their notes and can place them directly on the group's guided reading chart. You can save the notes after the lesson and use them to document your students' progress in strategy use.

After Reading: Question, Clarify, Summarize, and Check Predictions
Remember that the four reciprocal teaching strategies can be discussed in any order. However, I often use the following sequence because students are so enthusiastic about asking their questions after reading. Then, I alternate between modeling each strategy and allowing students to practice each one.

1. Model questioning for your students, and invite them to share their questions with partners or the group. As an option, write the questions on the guided reading chart that you have selected, or have your students write questions on self-stick notes to attach to the chart. Invite students to ask one another their questions.

   Encourage good social skills when the students are role-playing as teachers by praising correct answers and prompting incorrect or incomplete ones.

2. Refer to the predictions made prior to reading that are recorded on the chart, and model how to check a prediction to see if it came about or was changed during the reading. Have students take turns checking other predictions against what they have read.

3. Model one word or idea and how to clarify it. Have your students share their points to clarify and the strategies that they used for clarifying (refer to the Clarifying Bookmarks on page 95).

4. Either model a summary, guide the group in creating a summary, or invite individual students to summarize the text. Discuss any interesting text points and decide which ones belong in the summary.

   As an option, you can fill in the "What We Learned" column at this point if you have chosen to use the Know-Want-Learn Reciprocal Teaching Chart for Guided Reading on page 98.

5. For a fictional text, discuss any other points that you or students wish to talk about, including personal connections, character motives, favorite parts, surprises, and emotions.

   For nonfiction selections, reflect on the nonfiction text features—such as headings, maps, and visuals—and ask your students how they used the text features to help them understand the reading.

6. Ask your students to reflect on the four reciprocal teaching strategies, and invite them to tell the class which strategy helped them the most and why. Give examples and model reflection, if necessary.

Assessment Tips

- Keep your individual coaching notes and records of your observations of students during guided reading lessons by using the Reciprocal Teaching Observation Chart for Guided Reading (see chart on page 100). Use the rubrics in Appendix A (page 195) as an assessment guide.

- As you work your way through the lesson plan, have your students write some of their predictions, questions, points or words to clarify, and an occasional summary on either self-stick notes or forms from this book (such as the Literature Discussion Sheet for Reciprocal Teaching on page 141). Keep a guided reading observation notebook with one page designated for each student. After a lesson, remove any sticky notes initialed and dated by your students and place each one on the respective student's page in the notebook. Over time, your records will show how individual students have grown in their use of the four reciprocal teaching strategies. Then, you can form temporary groups of students who are having trouble with the same strategy or strategies and meet with the groups to teach more guided reading lessons or the minilessons on pages 124–127.

Clarifying Words Bookmark

1. Identify the difficult word.

The word _____
is tricky because

a. I had trouble pronouncing it.

b. I didn't know what it meant.

c. I didn't know what it meant, and I couldn't pronounce it.

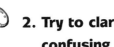 **2. Try to clarify the difficult word.**

I tried the following strategies to understand the difficult word:

____ I checked the parts of the word that I know (prefixes, suffixes, base words, and digraphs).

____ I tried blending the sounds of the word together.

____ I thought about where I have seen the word before.

____ I thought of another word that looks like this word.

____ I read on to find clues.

____ I tried another word that makes sense in the sentence.

____ I reread the sentence to see if the word I figured out made sense.

Clarifying Ideas Bookmark

1. Identify the confusing part, which might be a sentence, paragraph, page, or chapter.

A confusing part is

_____

_____

because

a. I didn't understand _____.

b. I can't figure out _____.

c. It doesn't make sense.

d. I don't get _____.

e. This part isn't clear because _____.

2. Try to clarify the confusing part.

I tried the following strategies to understand the confusing part:

____ I reread the parts that I didn't understand and some text before that part.

____ I read on to look for clues.

____ I thought about what I know about the topic.

____ I talked to a friend about the reading.

Basic Comprehension Chart
for Guided Reading Groups

What We Know
(our experiences, background knowledge, and/or connections with the text)

Our Predictions
(make predictions before reading and check their accuracy after reading)

Our Questions
(who, when, what, where, why, how, and what if)

Our Words or Ideas to Clarify	How We Clarified

Our Summary

Reciprocal Teaching Guided Reading Nonfiction Chart

What We Know About
(Look at the book's cover and a few illustrations.)
Attach self-stick notes in the book, or write what we know in the space below.
Option: Categorize notes and label the categories.

What We Might Learn
(Look at the cover.)
I think we will learn...

Our Questions Before Reading
(Use a picture or text preview to create questions.)

Our Questions
(Create questions to ask one another after reading the text.)

Our Summary

Know-Want-Learn Reciprocal Teaching Chart
for Guided Reading

*What We Know About*_____

What We Want to Know—Our Questions (Preview pictures for each portion of text.)	What We Learned (Discuss and summarize what you learned from that portion of text before reading further.)
Before reading Preview illustrations and text pages ____ to ____ _____ _____ _____	**After reading** Reread quickly and summarize these pages. _____ _____ _____
Before reading Preview illustrations/text pages ____ to ____ _____ _____ _____	**After reading** Reread quickly and summarize these pages. _____ _____ _____
Before reading Preview illustrations/text pages ____ to ____ _____ _____ _____	**After reading** Reread quickly and summarize these pages. _____ _____ _____

Sources: Adapted from Ogle, D. (1986). K-W-L: A teaching model that develops active reading of expository text. *The Reading Teacher, 39*, 564–570.
Adapted from Cooper, J.D., Boschken, I., McWilliams, J., & Pistochini, L. (1997). *A study of effectiveness of an intervention program designed to accelerate reading for struggling readers in the upper grades.* Unpublished report.

Story Map Prediction Chart

Before Reading (Use text and illustrations to predict.)	**After Reading** (Fill in what actually happened.)
Setting:	Setting:
Characters:	Characters:
Problem:	Problem:
Main Events:	Main Events:
Resolution/Ending:	Resolution/Ending:
Theme or Lesson:	Theme or Lesson:

Source: Adapted from Hammond, D. (1991). Prediction chart. In J.M. Macon, D. Bewell, & M. Vogt, *Responses to literature: Grades K–8* (pp. 11–12). Newark, DE: International Reading Association.

Reciprocal Teaching Observation Chart
for Guided Reading

Code for Reciprocal Teaching Strategies Coached P = *predict* Q = *question* S = *summarize* C = *clarify*					
Student Name					
1.	Date	Date	Date	Date	Date
2.	Date	Date	Date	Date	Date
3.	Date	Date	Date	Date	Date
4.	Date	Date	Date	Date	Date
5.	Date	Date	Date	Date	Date
6.	Date	Date	Date	Date	Date
7.	Date	Date	Date	Date	Date

Lesson 2: Using Comprehension Charts

 Predict　　 **Question**　　 **Clarify**　　 **Summarize**

Many students are visual learners who benefit greatly from the use of graphic organizers during instruction. I rely on teacher-created comprehension charts, such as the Basic Comprehension Chart for Guided Reading Groups (page 96), the Reciprocal Teaching Guided Reading Nonfiction Chart (page 97), the Know-Want-Learn Reciprocal Teaching Chart for Guided Reading (page 98), and the Story Map Prediction Chart (page 99), during guided reading lessons to help students monitor their comprehension and to guide the reciprocal teaching discussion. Although a comprehension chart is a concrete place for recording discussions, responses, and reflections, you also might include prior knowledge activation, predictions, student-generated questions, points to clarify, and a group summary on your class's comprehension chart. Depending on whether the genre is fiction or nonfiction, you can change the look of the chart. For example, for a story you might use the Story Map Prediction Chart (page 99), but when reading a nonfiction text you might use the Know-Want-Learn Reciprocal Teaching Chart for Guided Reading to record your students' learning (page 98). Although you can use such charts during whole-class instruction as well, I find that comprehension charts in general are especially effective for guiding small-group instruction because they assist students who need visual aids to guide their reading and boost their comprehension.

Because reciprocal teaching is a discussion technique, you should not require your students to write long pieces for the comprehension chart but only brief reminders on the self-stick notes. The notes give your students ownership of the chart and keep the focus on the discussion, not the written responses.

The logistics of where to place or hang a comprehension chart can be challenging, but there are some easy solutions. Use a whiteboard or chart paper on a stand if you can position it near the guided reading table. For settings where the reading table is a convenient place for hanging a chart, write on a large piece of construction paper or use a legal-size file folder to prop up your chart. I have found that, even if I quickly write on a chart with it flat on the table, the students in the group can see what I am writing. Even if my students and I are seated on the floor, I find a way to incorporate a comprehension chart of some kind, and you can, too. In addition, if you create the charts on legal-size folders or large sheets of construction paper, you can save and store them easily after the lesson.

This lesson includes several variations on comprehension charts (the Classroom Story on page 106 shows this lesson plan being taught with a story map). However, you can create new ones to use with each book that you read with a small group of students. The possibilities for comprehension charts are limitless. After including spaces on your chart for recording predictions, questions, clarifications, and summaries, you can add optional spaces for connections, reactions, wonder questions, opinions, and/or student drawings.

In this lesson,

- a written record of the reciprocal teaching strategies helps your students to remember and reflect on strategy use,

- visual reminders of the reading selection highlights help your students to summarize, and

- visual reminders of predictions help your students to monitor their comprehension as they read.

Remind your students that there are other strategies that good readers use such as visualizing and self-questioning (Keene & Zimmermann, 1997; McLaughlin & Allen, 2002; Pearson et al., 1992). When appropriate, create space on your class's comprehension charts for other strategy notes (for example, inferences, connections, and visualized concepts).

Materials

- Paper to use for the comprehension chart—either chart paper, a whiteboard, or large sheets of butcher or construction paper

- A supply of pencils, markers, self-stick notes, and tape

- Any of the following charts from this book:
  Basic Comprehension Chart for Guided Reading Groups (page 96)
  Reciprocal Teaching Guided Reading Nonfiction Chart (page 97)
  Know-Want-Learn Reciprocal Teaching Chart for Guided Reading (page 98)
  Story Map Prediction Chart (page 99)

1. Select a text to use with your reciprocal teaching guided reading group. You may group particular students together because they need work on the same strategy, are at the same reading level, or have selected the same text to read. (See pages 80–82 for more information on forming groups.)

2. Sketch a comprehension chart in front of your students, using one of the recommended charts or your own chart. Be sure to allow a place for jotting down notes about what your students already know and/or connections that they make to the text, and also include places for noting predictions, questions, clarifications, and summaries.

   Tell your students that they will use the chart to guide them through that day's reading and will return to it in subsequent meetings.

3. Model how your students can make connections to and predictions about the text and use their background knowledge by previewing the text and noting a connection and a prediction on self-stick notes.

   Use these self-stick notes and others created by your students to fill in the experiences, connections, or "What We Know (About)" portion and the predictions portion of the chosen chart before reading the text.

1. Ask your students to read the text silently after they have added their predictions, connections, and experiences to the chart or you have written them on the chart. You can ask the students who finish early to each reread the text and write a question for the group to answer. Another option for early finishers is to have other reading material available at the guided reading table.

2. Model the reciprocal teaching strategies one at a time, and ask your students to follow your example. For instance, when all students have finished reading, discuss their predictions first. Discuss whether they changed their predictions while reading. Then, model a question and ask your students to ask questions of their own. (Students usually love asking questions first, so let them do it.) Have them record one question each on a self-stick note for the chart.

Then, model a clarification and ask your students to come up with clarifications of their own. They may also write their clarification points on self-stick notes for the chart.

Finally, model a summary and then ask the group to help you summarize. Record the group's summary on the comprehension chart. See Figures 19 and 20 for examples of comprehension charts completed by students.

3. Continue to use modeling throughout many reciprocal teaching sessions, but gradually release the responsibility to your students. For example, invite student volunteers to model the first prediction, question, clarification, or summary.

4. Ask your students to discuss how reciprocal teaching strategies helped them to comprehend the text during the lesson.

Assessment Tips

- When your students contribute to a comprehension chart, have them put their names or initials on their responses. If you are taking dictation of their discussions, simply write the students' initials next to their responses. This way, you can make notes to yourself and keep track of individual students' progress during reciprocal teaching discussions. You might choose to transfer the self-stick notes used on the chart to a page for each child in a guided reading observation notebook.

- Do not judge your students' writing skills based on their comprehension chart responses. Remember that the chart is a discussion guide and a visual reminder for students, not a writing assessment. Instead, look for the quality of their responses as they use each reciprocal teaching strategy.

- When coaching individual students, use the coaching prompts in Figure 18 (page 89) to help you to guide your students to use the four reciprocal teaching strategies more effectively.

- If your students are having difficulty clarifying ideas, be sure to continue modeling at least one point to clarify per session or text. Discuss how to clarify ideas by using the Clarifying Bookmarks (page 95). Emphasize rereading as an effective clarifying strategy.

Figure 19
A Guided Reading Chart About Spiders, Completed by a Second-Grade Guided Reading Group

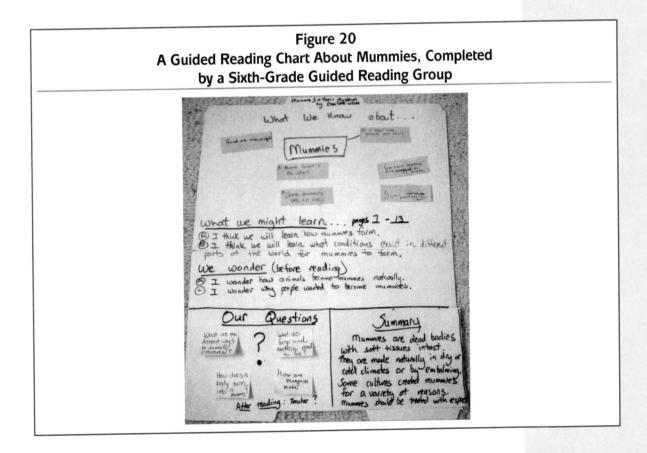

Figure 20
A Guided Reading Chart About Mummies, Completed by a Sixth-Grade Guided Reading Group

- If your students are having trouble summarizing on their own, summarize as a group. Then, student pairs can work together to reiterate the summary. Watch for word-for-word text retellings, and encourage your students to use their own words when they summarize.

- Form temporary, flexible strategy groups of students that may need to work on one particular strategy or all four. Teach the minilessons at the end of this chapter (pages 124–127) to students who need extra support. Also, refer to Figure 4 (page 21) when your students struggle.

Guiding Comprehension With a Story Map Chart During Guided Reading for Grade 4

The fourth graders in Ms. Garcia's classroom select books that they want to read and form mixed-ability groups based on interest in the same book. The class meets in literature circles first, and I call up one or two of the circles per day to work with me in a guided reading group. I rarely see teachers using literature circles as a classroom management tool during guided reading sessions, but it works well with intermediate students who have been trained in literature circle procedures. In classrooms in which students have not had literature circle training, I have the rest of the class engage in independent work such as reading self-selected books, writing in journals, or reading with partners.

The group I am meeting with today is reading the picture book *JoJo's Flying Side Kick* (Pinkney, 1999). The group members have selected this text because they will read it with their little buddies from a first-grade class with whom they meet every Friday.

Before Reading: Making Connections and Predicting   First, I ask the students what they think the book will be about. "I can tell by the cover that it is about a girl who is in tae kwon do," says Kris. "I take tae kwon do on Tuesdays," comments Tomás. The students talk about connections that the text has to their lives. I add, "Good readers naturally make connections when they read. You are making personal or text-to-self connections to the topic before we read. What else can you say about the topic of tae kwon do to help activate your prior knowledge?" The students briefly share their experiences with taking martial arts classes or watching martial arts programs on television.

I ask the students to turn to a partner and take a picture walk through the text while making predictions. After the picture walk, I ask the students to identify some words that may appear in the text and write the words on self-stick notes. They write words such as *yellow belt*, *promotion*, and *congratulations*.

Tomás and Kris disappointedly tell me that the other pairs have taken their ideas for words. I redirect their attention to several of the illustrations and ask them to think about the feelings that JoJo might be having. "She looks worried and nervous," interjects Kris.

"How do you know?" I ask. "Because her face just looks worried," adds Tomás. The pair decides to write the word *nervous* on their self-stick note.

We post the self-stick notes on a chart, and I ask the students to watch the text for these words or words with similar meanings. Then, I write the story map elements on the chart and ask the students to predict *where* the setting is, *who* the characters are, *what* the problem is, and *what* events may occur. They offer the following ideas:

"The setting is at the tae kwon do center and JoJo's house."

"The characters are the grandfather, JoJo, the tae kwon do teacher, and JoJo's mom."

When I ask the students to predict what the problem in the story might be, the students stop to think, and I wait. Ben predicts, "I think that she will not pass the test the first time to get her next belt." The group is satisfied with that idea. I prompt them a bit, asking, "What about the way she feels? Could feelings be a problem, too?" Hands go up. Ben adds, "I think she will be nervous. It is hard to do a good job when you are too nervous." The students nod in agreement, and several of them share times when they were nervous about a sporting competition or performance.

I tell the group that after reading we will return to the predictions to see how accurate they were. I also tell them that it is very natural for readers to change their predictions as they read and learn more about what really happens in the story.

During Reading: Clarifying   The students read silently, and I rotate around the group, asking each student to read aloud to me. I decide to focus my attention on the clarifying strategy as I coach each student individually.

When I get to Alexandra, I ask her to tell me if there are any parts or words in the story that she needs to clarify. "I don't know what *promotion* means," admits Alexandra. "I'm so glad that you can find a word that you did not understand. How can you clarify the meaning of that word?" I respond. "I can reread," she offers (she rereads the sentence with the word *promotion* in it). "Now do you know what it means?" I ask. "Not really, " she admits. "What else could you do to figure it out? Look at your Clarifying Words Bookmark," I prompt. "I could read on to find clues?" she answers shyly. We read on together, and Alexandra beams as she tells me that she thinks *promotion* means that JoJo gets to go to the next level or get her next belt. I praise her and tell her that she is a super clarifier. As I continue rotating to each student to ask him or her to find a word or idea to clarify, I direct each one's attention to the Clarifying Bookmarks for strategies to use when clarifying.

Some students finish reading early, and I ask them to practice reading the text with a partner and with expression because they will read the book to their second-grade buddies in a few days. Also, I give them self-stick notes to mark the text in spots where they will ask the little buddies questions and whether they need to clarify any words or ideas. "I am going to mark *promotion* and ask my buddy if he knows what it means. If he doesn't, I'll help him clarify," adds Alexandra proudly.

After Reading: Summarizing   First, I ask the students to return to the chart and write the story elements—setting, characters, the problem, events, and ending—on new self-stick notes, which I will place next to their original predictions about story elements. They discuss their original predictions and the actual setting, characters, problem, and events. We look at the list of words that they thought might be in the selection. The students feel proud that most of those words, or at least words that mean the same things, were in the selection.

Because summarizing is always difficult for students, I model how to summarize by using the story map as a guide. Then, I shorten my verbal summary and show the students how to make it even shorter while still including necessary information:

> *JoJo's Flying Side Kick* is about a girl who is nervous about passing the test for her yellow belt in tae kwon do. Family members and friends give her advice to pass such as doing a shuffle step for nervousness, yelling for a power kick, and visualizing her technique. JoJo uses their advice and passes the test.

Then, I ask students at the table to pair up and use the story map chart as a guide as they take turns summarizing on their own. I ask the students to think about the book's theme and to be prepared for the next time we meet to discuss connections that they made to the text.

Tomás raises his hand. He says, "I know what the lesson is. To succeed, you can prepare and ask for advice!" I ask the other students in the group if they agree, and they nod. I invite them to think more about the story's theme and suggest that we meet one more time to discuss the theme and how their little buddies will use reciprocal teaching strategies when we meet with them on Friday.

Before leaving the guided reading table, the students share with a partner which strategy helped them the most today.

"Predicting was useful today because I had to keep thinking about what the main character, JoJo, would do next," offers Kelly.

"I clarified some words I didn't know," adds Tomás.

Reflection and Next Steps   In the next session, the students will share how the buddies did when using the four reciprocal teaching strategies with this book. They will discuss which strategies the buddies used well and which ones gave them the most trouble. I also will encourage the fourth graders to practice their summaries once again, using the Story Map Chart as a guide. Then, they will try to shorten their summaries without referring to the chart. Finally, we will discuss the themes of lessons that the fourth graders derived from the book.

Lesson 3: Coaching Students in Reciprocal Teaching During Guided Reading

Predict

Question

Clarify

Summarize

During guided reading sessions, I tell the students that I work with that I am similar to a coach who compliments them and gives helpful hints as they, the athletes, play the game of reading. Sometimes during guided reading lessons, I wear a hat or visor that says *Coach* on it to illustrate the point that the students are doing the work with my guidance. Students love this real-life comparison.

So, how can you effectively coach individual students in reciprocal teaching strategies during a guided reading group? Picture the coaching sessions in this lesson in a spot that makes sense in your classroom. Perhaps you meet with small groups at a kidney-shaped table with you seated on the inside. Maybe you are into less formal settings for reading groups and meet with students on a rug or in beanbag chairs. Either way, the physical arrangement of the setting is important to conducting this lesson. It is helpful to read with and coach each student privately without interrupting the other students as they read silently.

If you work at a kidney-shaped table with your students, move from the table's center to the outside. Then, sit or crouch next to each student for just a few moments to check his or her use of one reciprocal teaching strategy and provide necessary guidance before moving to coach the next student. You may not make it to every student in the group during one lesson, but you can make a note of which students need to be coached during the next lesson. By moving around the outside of the table to work with your students, you can keep the coaching sessions quiet.

This lesson offers prompts to use for each of the reciprocal teaching strategies during guided reading sessions. (The Classroom Story on page 113 shows this lesson plan in action.) Use the prompts with individual students and keep track of your coaching sessions using the Reciprocal Teaching Observation Chart for Guided Reading (page 100). During this lesson,

- your students are held individually accountable for one of the four reciprocal teaching strategies,

- your students verbalize a think-aloud for the reciprocal teaching strategies, and

- you provide a model for or guide each student in the reciprocal teaching strategies.

Materials

- Multiple copies of reading material for a small group of students
- Multiple copies of the Be the Teacher Bookmark (page 53) with reciprocal teaching strategies for student and teacher reference
- List of coaching prompts from Figure 18 (page 89)
- Reciprocal Teaching Observation Chart for Guided Reading (page 100)

Teacher Modeling

1. Begin the guided reading group by introducing a new book or, if your class is already engaged in a text, by reviewing what the group has read so far. Preview the portion of text that the group will read during this lesson by looking at headings and illustrations and making predictions.

   If the text has no illustrations, then read aloud the first few paragraphs and skim over each page for vocabulary that stands out. Have your students write predictions about the text on self-stick notes, and post the notes on the group's comprehension chart.

2. Review all reciprocal teaching strategies, or focus on one strategy. Quickly model each strategy, using examples from the text that the group is reading.

   When you focus on one particular strategy, ask your students to closely observe your think-aloud. Tell them that they will have a chance to practice the strategy or strategies with you as you coach individual students.

3. As you move around the group, choose strategies to coach based on any of the following criteria:

   - Coach all students on the focus strategy that you taught in the minilesson prior to reading

- Coach each student on a strategy that you think he or she needs to practice based on your previous observations
- Ask your students which strategy they want to practice or demonstrate for you

4. If a student needs to be coached on a particular reciprocal teaching strategy, provide a model of that strategy and ask him or her to try again with the next paragraph or page of the text.

   Give the student specific examples such as "I noticed that you were having trouble with summarizing this page. I can model that for you so you can see how to summarize. Watch how I tell the events in order. Also, I reread the paragraph to remember all the main points. You can try summarizing again with the next page." Coach a few students that day and the rest the following day. If your students are done reading silently, and you have not coached everyone, then you can coach the students that you missed the next time they meet in a guided reading group.

Student Participation

1. Have your students begin to read silently, and tell them that you will coach them in their use of reciprocal teaching strategies. Select a student to work with, and sit next to him or her. Ask the student to read a sentence or two aloud. Then, either you or the student can select a reciprocal teaching strategy for him or her to model.

2. Ask a student to work on one reciprocal teaching strategy in the portion of text that he or she is currently reading. Then, use one of the prompts in Figure 18 on page 89 to help the student get started with the chosen strategy.

3. When the student finishes modeling the reciprocal teaching strategy, give him or her very specific compliments such as "I like the way that you used clues from the heading to make a logical prediction" or "That question is one that I had to use several clues from the text to answer. Good job!"

- Use the rubric in Appendix A (page 195) for guidelines on each reciprocal teaching strategy.

- Take notes on individual students during guided silent reading and group discussions, marking which strategies the students demonstrate and a few notes about what they do. The following list provides some examples.

> Oct. 8—Juan summarized the paragraph on page 1. Left out two of the five main ideas.
>
> Sam clarified the word *follow* by making an analogy to the word *swallow*.
>
> Rachael asked a literal question about page 13.

Use your notes to guide the next few lessons. Which strategies do your students need to work on the most?

- Use the information that you gather on the Reciprocal Teaching Observation Chart for Guided Reading (page 100) to help you flexibly group students according to their strategy use. Form student groups and teach focus lessons or minilessons on the strategies with which the students are having trouble.

- Provide support for students when they need reinforcement by teaching the following lessons in guided reading groups:

> Minilessons for Reciprocal Teaching With Guided Reading Groups (pages 124–127)
>
> Using Movie or Television Clips and Freeze Frames to Retell and Summarize lesson (page 116)
>
> Using the Clarifying Bookmarks lesson (page 121)

- Check each student's ability to use the strategies in concert. Have each student read a passage and verbally give you a response for each strategy. Use Figure 4 (page 21) for additional suggestions when your students struggle with a specific strategy.

- Ask students to self-assess by asking themselves, Which strategies are helping me the most? and Which strategies do I find myself using in other reading situations? Ask your students to give examples of how they use the strategies at home and when they are reading at their desks independently or with a partner.

Coaching Second-Grade Students During Guided Reading

On the day of the 2002 winter Olympics opening ceremonies, I find a treasure to use with groups of second graders during a guided reading lesson. The *Reading Safari Magazine* special edition on the Olympics (2001) has a table of contents listing nonfiction articles on the history of the Olympics, a fictional account of a family attending the opening ceremonies, poetry, a Readers Theatre activity, and an article about a website on the Olympics. I know it will take numerous visits with each guided reading group over the course of a week to finish the entire magazine.

For today's lesson, I choose the fictional piece "At the Opening Ceremony" (Tabakas, 2001). I tell the students that they will need to pay close attention to the story so they can stand in front of the television before the Olympics are broadcast that evening and teach their families at least five facts about the opening ceremonies. The second graders are anxious to read the article and become opening-ceremony experts.

In this particular second-grade classroom, the teacher—Mrs. Webster—meets regularly with two guided reading groups in the morning and two in the afternoon. Because I am working with the afternoon group, the lessons have to be interactive and high interest because the students are often tired or fidgety at the end of the day. While I meet with groups, the other students in the class are engaged in the following reading comprehension-building activities: reading the newspaper in pairs to look for Olympics-related news, reading their self-selected books, or writing journal entries in response to a story from the district-adopted anthology.

The first mixed-ability, guided reading group of six students and I prepare to create a comprehension chart together. Many students are visual learners, so I always use a minichart during guided reading lessons. Throughout the lessons, I write on the chart or have students write on self-stick notes and place them on the chart. The chart helps focus the learning on the strategies we are using, and I save the charts from lesson to lesson to jog the students' memories.

Before Reading: Background Building and Prediction

I begin the lesson by asking the six students what good readers do before reading a text. Robbie answers, "They think about what they know about the topic, and they predict." Then, I ask the students what they know about the Olympics. They give me blank stares, so I try a strategy to refresh their memories. "You may take the magazine, and I will give you one minute to page through its pictures," I explain. The students quickly page through the magazine, and when they close the last page I ask them to turn to a partner and tell that person what they know about the Olympics. The comments follow:

"I know people win gold medals," comments Rachael.

"Greece comes in first in the opening ceremonies," Nicola, whose family is from Greece, announces with pride.

"The events are different for summer and winter Olympics," comments Bryce.

After this quick discussion, I pass out brightly colored self-stick notes and ask each student to take a pencil and write down two things that they know about the Olympics. I tell them to get their ideas down quickly and not to worry about spelling. The purpose of their jotting quick notes now is to access their prior knowledge, and I do not want them to lose their thoughts and ideas. Later, if we save the chart and use it for reference, I will ask students to help me find misspellings and correct them. They write on their self-stick notes:

> The opening sarimony is when all the state's come out in abc order and they cary their flags.
>
> I know that they do sports and they compet with other countries.
>
> The Olympics started in Greece.

After this activity, I hold up my copy of the magazine and encourage the students to look at its cover. I ask them, "What do you think you will learn from reading this magazine?" The students answer, and I write their comments on the chart, placing their initials next to their ideas.

> A. I think I will learn where the Olympics started.
> B. I think I will learn what events are in the Olympics.
> R. I think I will learn what the torch looks like.
> P. I think I will learn what they do at the opening ceremonies.

One student, Marina, sits quietly when it is her turn to contribute to the discussion. When she shrugs her shoulders and says that she does not know what she will learn, I open the magazine to the first page of the opening ceremonies article and ask Marina to tell me what she sees. She says, "I see a crowd of people waiting for the Olympics." "What do you think you might learn from this page? What do you think the author will say about this picture? The title 'At the Opening Ceremony' might help you, too," I prompt. After a brief silence, Marina comments in a questioning tone, "I will learn that lots of people go to the Olympics?" I compliment her on using the clues from the article's title and picture to help her make a prediction about what she will learn, and I add her prediction to the chart.

Next, I engage the students in a picture walk (Clay, 1985): I hold up my text and we look at its captions, illustrations, and photos to discuss concepts and vocabulary. I ask the students to keep in mind that after the picture walk, they will write on self-stick notes the questions that they have about the Olympics.

After the picture walk, the students ask questions such as, "How long are the opening ceremonies?" "Who started the Olympics?" "What events are in the decathlon?" Pablo says that he does not have a question, so I direct his attention to the photograph on page 16 of the text of the runners bringing in the torch. "Do you wonder anything about this photograph? What would you like to know?" I ask. "I wonder how far the relay runners go," he says. I compliment his effort, "Good, I like the way you studied the photo and came up with a question that may be answered when we read," then add his question to our chart.

During Reading: Coaching Students   Next, I ask the students to read the article about the opening ceremony and keep in mind their questions and what they think they will learn. Also, I tell them that they will read the text two times—once to enjoy it and once to think of a question to ask the group.

While the students read silently, I circulate around the outside of the kidney-shaped table to ask each student to read a paragraph or two for me. Each student has different needs, and I coach each one accordingly. I compliment Bryce's oral reading and ask him to cover the text and tell me in his own words what he just read. He has difficulty remembering, so I ask him to quickly reread the page again. This time, he smiles as he executes a more complete summary. I move on to Rachael and ask her to make up a question about the page that she just read. She asks, "What do the rings on the Olympic flag stand for?" I praise her excellent question. Last, I ask Marina if there are any difficult words in what she read and, if so, how she figured them out. She points to *declared* and says that she figured out how to say it by looking for parts that she knew such as *de* and *clar* and putting them together to make *declared*. I ask her if she knows what the word means, and she shrugs her shoulders. Together, we reread the sentence and decide that it means that the games were officially starting.

After Reading: Returning to Predictions, Asking Questions, and Summarizing

After the students finish reading and have their questions ready to ask the group, I ask them all to refer to what they thought they would learn and the questions that they formed before reading. Then, the students pose their questions to the group. As each student speaks, I encourage the other students to look at the "teacher." The students ask their questions and call on eager hand-raisers to answer them. The teacher for the moment praises or coaches the student who answers with comments such as "Right!" "Good job!" or "Try again."

To finish the lesson, I write numbers 1–5 on the chart and ask the students to help me to collect five important ideas from the text that they could tell their families prior to watching the opening ceremonies that night. As they dictate, I write their facts:

1. The torch comes in with runners.
2. The Olympics started in Greece, so Greece always goes first.
3. The countries come in alphabetical order.
4. The rings stand for five continents.
5. The athletes take the Olympic oath.

Before the six students leave the table to make and decorate their own summary sheets, complete with drawings and the five facts, they each have to tell me which strategies helped them the most today. Bryce says, "Summarizing helped because I want to teach my family about the opening ceremony." Rachael adds, "I liked the five summary points because they helped me to summarize." Marina comments, "Looking through the pictures helped me predict today."

Reflection and Next Steps
The next time we meet, the students will discuss the opening ceremonies that they viewed on television. For the next few class sessions, the teacher and I will work on creating more guided reading charts with the group using nonfiction texts, activating students' prior knowledge, listing questions prior to reading, and writing five main points for a summary.

Lesson 4: Using Movie or Television Clips and Freeze Frames to Retell and Summarize

Summarize

Background and Description

Often, when asked to summarize a story or nonfiction text, children lapse into a long litany of events linked together with a seemingly endless series of *and thens*. When our students can retell stories in great detail, we teachers are thrilled because as students do so, they exhibit many important skills, including sequencing, using story language, and recalling events. However, we also need to teach our students various skills to move them toward shorter retellings and briefer summaries.

I like to help students recognize that summarizing and retelling are two different strategies that require some of the same skills. I think of summarizing and retelling as cousins because they are from the same family of comprehension strategies but look a bit different. A retelling is longer and more detailed than a summary, whereas a summary is short and to the point—a bare-bones recounting of the text. It is important for students to recognize the differences and similarities between summarizing and retelling so they can learn to generate both correctly.

This lesson includes some entertaining ways for students to practice verbal retellings and summaries of popular movies and television programs. During this lesson, you will teach your students that a retelling is like a series of movie clips, not the entire full-length movie. Then, you will talk to your students about short movie reviews that are found in the newspaper and on the news and explain that a summary is like a series of freeze frames that give only the most essential information about a movie or television show. You also can model for students how to summarize fiction and nonfiction texts by discussing summaries of fictional movies and nonfiction television programs.

The ideas in this lesson should be taught over several days during guided reading sessions. The lesson could be presented to the entire class, but my experience has been that students grasp and retain the information much better by working on summarizing and retelling in a small-group format. Students will learn to

- recognize retellings and summaries,
- retell and summarize main ideas and events in a logical order,
- reread a text to review it before retelling or summarizing, and
- read real-world movie and television reviews.

Materials

See Figure 21 for materials and instructions on creating movie or television clips and freeze frames.

Teacher Modeling

1. Model a retelling of a children's movie. If you are retelling a movie that is still in theaters, bring in a newspaper review of the movie and discuss any pertinent background information. Give details, describe scenes, reiterate dialogue from the movie, retell events in order, and provide main ideas. Tell your students to try to visualize the action as you retell the story.

2. Model a summary of the same movie. Begin by telling your students that you are only giving four sentences—or freeze frames—from the movie, not a series of detailed movie clips like in the retelling. Offer three to four sentences using guide words such as *first, next, then,* and *finally*. Include information about the characters, the problem, one or two key events, the ending, and the main ideas.

Student Participation

1. Compare and contrast summarizing and retelling in a discussion. Draw a chart (see below) with *retelling/movie clips* in one column and *summarizing/freeze frames* in the other.

Retelling/Movie Clips
What do you notice?
Include
- details,
- dialogue,
- events in order,
- description, and
- main ideas and details.

Summarizing/Freeze Frames
What do you notice?
Include
- words such as *first, next, then,* and *finally*;
- the characters, problem, main events in order, and ending; and
- the main ideas.

Figure 21
**How to Create Movie or Television Clips and Freeze Frames
to Retell and Summarize**

Retelling: Make Movie or Television Clips	Summarizing: Make Freeze Frames

Retelling: Make Movie or Television Clips

Materials
- An empty cardboard box
- Adding-machine tape or scrap paper
- Butcher paper
- Clear or masking tape
- Two paper tubes
- Crayons, markers, or paints
- Scissors

Directions

1. Use an empty box to make a television or movie screen by making slits with scissors across from one another on the vertical sides of the box.

2. Plan your retelling on a piece of adding-machine tape or scrap paper.

3. Then, draw with crayons, markers, or paint a retelling of your reading on a piece of butcher paper that will fit through the slits that you made in the sides of the cardboard box.

4. Slide the butcher paper into one of the slits and position it so an image fits in the "screen" at the front of the box. Figure out a way for the show to move across the screen as you share your retelling. Either attach the paper tubes to either end of the butcher paper or have a student pull the paper through the slits at the proper times.

Option: Make a teeny, tiny movie retelling by using a small cardboard box and adding-machine tape.

Summarizing: Make Freeze Frames

Materials
- Overhead projector transparencies
- Overhead transparency markers
- Overhead projector

Directions

1. Plan your summary using only one to three overhead projector transparencies.

2. Using the markers, draw freeze frames that illustrate your summary on the transparencies.

3. Share your freeze-frame summary with the class by using the overhead projector.

Note: Instead of making one of these projects, you may wish to make a movie or television clip retelling or freeze-frame summary using your computer and any special software that you have available.

Reciprocal Teaching at Work: Strategies for Improving Reading Comprehension by Lori D. Oczkus © 2003. Newark, DE: International Reading Association. May be copied for classroom use.

Ask your students to tell you what they noticed about your retelling and summary. Use the chart to record your students' responses and guide future retellings and summaries.

2. Guide your students in selecting a movie and retelling the story as a group. You may wish to record the retelling on a chart.

3. Guide your students in shortening their group retelling into a brief summary. You may wish to underline key parts of the retelling on the chart and then rewrite them into a summary.

4. Model retelling and summarizing, and guide your students in these skills using familiar folk tales and grade-level texts. Ask your students to observe as you give a retelling of a familiar folk tale such as *Little Red Hen* or *Goldilocks and the Three Bears*. Include details and dialogue in your retelling. Summarize the same story using three or four sentences, then invite your students to help you do the same with another folk tale.

Or, model for your students a retelling of a book that they have read recently. Emphasize the importance of rereading and reviewing the text in order to remember the reading. Summarize the same text, then invite your students to assist you in retelling and summarizing another book that the group has read before. Encourage student pairs to retell and summarize books that the class has read.

5. Have several students in the guided reading group write a retelling of a movie, and run a long piece of paper through a cardboard box that is fashioned to look like a television. Some students also may enjoy making tiny movies with adding-machine tape or making freeze-frame summaries by drawing on transparencies cut into any size.

An optional fun idea is to provide plastic microphones for your students to use as they act as television reporters while giving their retellings and summaries.

- Ask your students to reflect on the differences between retelling and summarizing. How does each strategy help them to understand what they read?

- Can your students engage in effective retellings and summaries? When they summarize, are they able to give only key events without including too many details? Do they summarize in order and in their own words? Do they reread or use text illustrations while preparing a retelling or summary? When your students struggle with retelling or summarizing, be sure to model these skills for them, or invite students who summarize well to provide models for the group.

- Limit the number of sheets of paper or transparencies that your students can use so they will create shorter summaries.

- Teach the Partner Page Summary minilesson (page 127) at the guided reading table. Guide students as they work with partners to take turns summarizing each page of a text. When necessary, model how to summarize.

- If your students are struggling with developing summaries on their own, try having partners write summaries together and share their work with the guided reading group. Then, have the group vote on the summary that they think is on target in length and content. Have your students assist you in making a list of what makes a good summary.

- Encourage your students to illustrate their summaries to demonstrate their thinking and promote knowledge retention.

- Do your students naturally move into a discussion of the story theme? Ask them to offer a quick thought about the theme of the text that you have read.

Lesson 5: Using the Clarifying Bookmarks

Clarify

I started a tradition with one of my intervention groups that I have incorporated into all my guided reading groups. Each time the struggling fourth graders in Mrs. Williamson's class were excused from my guided reading table, their tickets to go back to their seats were to answer the question, "Which of the Fabulous Four did you use the most today and why? Give an example." Although most students varied their responses from day to day, Karen—the reader who struggled the most—chose the clarify strategy every day. At first, she could not give details about clarifying, and she said things such as, "Clarify helped me figure out the word *karate*" or "I sounded out the word *hibernate*." I decided that we needed bookmarks for Karen and all the students to use as they clarified both words and ideas (see the Clarifying Bookmarks on page 95). In addition to a bookmark including detailed prompts for clarifying words, I developed the Clarifying Ideas Bookmark with some prompts for clarifying ideas in a difficult portion of text, whether it be a sentence, page, or paragraph. I began using the bookmarks to guide me in making the strategies for clarifying more concrete.

The Clarifying Bookmarks proved to be effective tools. Not long after I introduced them, Karen began referring to them to explain in detail why she chose clarifying as the strategy that helped her the most. In fact, when the intervention group helped me to introduce reciprocal teaching strategies to the whole class, I invited the students in Karen's group to model each strategy. Of course, there was no doubt in my mind who would volunteer to be the clarifier. Using her Clarifying Bookmarks as a guide, Karen successfully modeled how to clarify.

How thrilling it is when students like Karen begin to understand and use the clarifying strategies to unlock words while they read. However, because clarifying is more than just clarifying words, you also must model techniques for clarifying unclear ideas in a text. It is common for students not to realize that they have missed something in their reading (Hacker & Tenent, 2002). By providing continuous modeling and using the prompts on the Clarifying Bookmarks, you can help your students see where they have experienced difficulties in understanding the text and teach them how to clarify ideas. This lesson includes suggestions for effectively using the Clarifying Bookmarks with your students and helps students with

- identifying words or ideas to clarify,
- using strategies for clarifying word meanings,
- choosing strategies for decoding words,
- using strategies for clarifying unclear ideas, and
- reflecting on clarifying strategies.

Remind your students that clarifying strategies fit into the broader list of comprehension strategies that good readers use to understand text such as visualizing and evaluating (Keene & Zimmermann, 1997; McLaughlin & Allen, 2002; Pearson et al., 1992).

Materials

- Multiple copies of reading material for the guided reading group
- A copy of the Clarifying Bookmarks (page 95) for each student (lamination and color printing are optional)

Teacher Modeling

1. Ask your students if they ever get stuck either on a hard word or a confusing part of a text when they are reading. Provide one or two examples of difficult words or ideas from their recent reading assignments.

   Ask your students what they know about clarifying, and tell them that you have a tool that will help them to remember and use clarifying strategies as they read.

2. Choose several words as examples from a text that your students have read. Use the Clarifying Words Bookmark, and tell them that it is not sufficient to identify a difficult word. The next step is to choose a clarifying strategy or two that will help them decipher the word.

   Have all the students find a particular word in the text and put their fingers under it as you model clarification steps. You may want to give each student a self-stick note or index card to place under the word. Then, choose another example, and clarify the word as a group.

3. Choose several ideas from the text that require clarifying strategies. Model how a reader might need to clarify the confusing parts of a text even though he or she may know all the words. Make sure that your students have copies of the text and are looking at the correct portion of text as you model clarifying. Model clarifying with at least one word and idea per reciprocal teaching session.

Student Participation

1. Choose several examples of words to clarify and ask the guided reading group to look on the Clarifying Words Bookmark and choose which strategies they think will work to clarify the word.

2. Choose a couple difficult or confusing paragraphs from texts that your students have read. Ask the guided reading group to help you clarify the text selections by using strategies from the Clarifying Ideas Bookmark.

3. Ask your students to reflect on the clarifying strategies on the Clarifying Bookmarks. Discuss which ones they found to be most helpful. Encourage them to use the bookmarks during independent reading.

Assessment Tips

- Use the Clarifying Bookmarks as you coach individual students. Which strategies are the students choosing the most? Prompt them to use other ones.
- Can your students verbalize the strategies that they use to clarify?
- Are your students clarifying ideas? Continue to model clarifying for them. Use the Clarifying Ideas Bookmark to prompt and guide them to find ideas to clarify and determine how to clarify those ideas.
- Are your students using rereading as a clarifying strategy for both words and ideas? If not, encourage them to do so. Make a poster for the classroom that says, "Reread, Reread, Reread!"
- Teach the Creating a Group Clarify Poster minilesson (page 126) for students who need extra support in using the clarify strategy.

Minilesson: Predicting With the Table of Contents

Description and Comprehension Strategies

Using a text that has a table of contents, have your students make predictions about the text based on its chapter titles. Comprehension strategies include predicting by using clues in the text.

Materials

multiple copies of a text that has a table of contents, self-stick notes, and a chart

Teacher Modeling

Select either a fiction or nonfiction text that has a table of contents. First, model predicting by using the cover; then, model predicting by using clues in the table of contents.

Student Participation

1. Invite your students to work in pairs to come up with either written or verbal predictions based on the chapter titles. Either have all pairs work on the same chapter title prediction, or assign a different chapter title for each pair to use for a prediction.

2. Record the predictions on self-stick notes or on a chart for the students. Place students' initials next to their respective predictions. After reading, check which predictions were correct and which were changed.

Assessment Tip

Are your students using clues from the table of contents to form logical predictions about the reading? Continue modeling prediction and guiding students as they make predictions.

Minilesson: Questioning With the Table of Contents

Description and Comprehension Strategies

Conduct this lesson either before or after reading a chapter book with a table of contents. Have students study a table of contents and then ask them to create questions that may be answered in given chapters. Comprehension strategies include questioning before and after reading.

Materials

multiple copies of a fiction or nonfiction text that has a table of contents and self-stick notes

Teacher Modeling

1. Before reading, model for your students how readers should look at a table of contents and come up with questions that they would like to have answered while reading.

2. After reading, model for your students how readers should look at a table of contents and come up with questions about each chapter.

Student Participation

1. Before reading, have your students work in pairs to write on self-stick notes one question that they have about the chapter, using the table of contents to create the questions.

   Have the pairs share their questions with the group and have the rest of the group read the text to answer them. Post the questions on a chart.

2. After reading, have each student pair use the table of contents to write one question that is answered in each chapter. As the pairs share their questions with the class, have the rest of the class study the table of contents and determine which chapter would have the answer. Save the questions on the chart so students can use them in further research or you can use them for assessment purposes.

Assessment Tip

Are your students asking questions that fit the chapter and table of contents's clues? Continue modeling if students are not asking appropriate questions.

Minilesson: Creating a Group Clarify Poster

Description and Comprehension Strategies

The guided reading group keeps track of strategies for clarifying words and ideas on a chart. Comprehension strategies include plans for clarifying words and ideas while reading.

This minilesson can be taught over two days. If you do so, stop after the teacher modeling steps on the first day and continue on the second day with the student modeling steps.

Materials

multiple copies of the chosen text and chart paper (or a file folder to display the chart at the table)

Teacher Modeling

1. Make a two-column chart with the headings "Clarifying Words" and "Clarifying Ideas."

2. Ask your students what good readers do when they need to clarify a word. Give them examples, and also chart their own responses.

3. Model several of the students' responses.

4. Ask your students what good readers do when they need to clarify the meaning of an entire sentence, paragraph, page, or chapter. Give them examples of confusing ideas in texts, and also chart their own responses.

5. Model several of the students' responses.

Student Participation

1. After reading a selection, invite your students to put words that need to be clarified on self-stick notes along with at least two strategies that they used to figure them out. Place the self-stick notes on the chart.

2. After reading, invite your students to write on sticky notes for the chart any ideas that were confusing and the page numbers where the ideas can be found in the text. Discuss strategies for clarifying ideas, and place the suggestions on the chart.

Assessment Tip

Are your students using the clarification strategies in their own reading? As the group reads, watch to see if students refer to the poster on clarifying. Every time the guided reading group meets, choose one word and one idea from the reading to model clarifying strategies.

Minilesson: Partner Page Summary

Description and Comprehension Strategies

Students work in pairs and take turns reading a page and summarizing it. Comprehension strategies include summarizing by using vocabulary from the text and selecting main ideas.

Materials

multiple copies of the chosen text, overhead transparencies, and overhead transparency markers

Teacher Modeling

Model how to effectively summarize a page of text by rereading for main ideas. Place an overhead transparency over the text and, with an overhead transparency marker, circle three to five key words or underline key phrases to use in your model summary.

Student Participation

1. Ask your students to work in pairs to take turns rereading the text, underlining several key words, and giving a verbal summary for the page using those words.

2. Instruct them to erase the transparency page quickly after the first student's summary and exchange roles.

3. When your students do this activity during guided reading sessions, you can assist, guide, and observe their interactions.

Assessment Tip

Listen to the pairs as they summarize. Can they select main ideas and vocabulary from the text and incorporate these elements into brief summaries? Model summarizing again in a small-group setting for students who are having difficulty.

Adapted from a presentation by Linda Hoyt during the institute titled "Exploring Informational Texts Through Guided Reading and Writing" at the 47th Annual Convention of the International Reading Association, San Francisco, California, 2002.

- Reciprocal teaching strategies can enhance comprehension when they are taught during small-group, guided reading instruction. The small-group format allows for further scaffolding of the four reciprocal teaching strategies.

- Students have the opportunity to use reciprocal teaching strategies in a variety of texts including grade-level and leveled texts.

- Primary and intermediate intervention programs have influenced guided reading practices.

- Four main ways to group for guided reading are

  1. strategy needs groups based on which reciprocal teaching strategy students need to practice the most,

  2. student choice groups based on students having selected the same title,

  3. intervention groups for students who read below grade level and are struggling but who also are engaged in grade-level literature and other reciprocal teaching groups, and

  4. ability-level reading groups for students who read at the same reading level and are matched to a text that is at their level.

- A powerful intervention for struggling readers introduces them to reciprocal teaching strategies during guided reading instruction. After several months of using guided reading and reciprocal teaching with struggling students, you can have them introduce the reciprocal teaching strategies to the rest of the class. The intervention students become the resident experts during whole-class and literature circle lessons.

- Reciprocal teaching strategies can be taught to all students during their guided reading groups prior to using the strategies in other settings, such as literature circles.

- Comprehension charts are effective visual tools for monitoring and guiding students in using the four reciprocal teaching strategies.

- Lesson plans for guided reading with nonfiction include previewing and discussing the nonfiction text features such as headings and illustrations.

- Assessment procedures during guided reading include observing, coaching individual students, reflecting on strategy use, and collecting brief written responses from students for a chart or discussion purposes.

Reflections for Group Study, Self-Study, or Staff Development

1 How do reciprocal teaching strategies fit into guided reading lesson plans for fiction and nonfiction?

2 What are some ways to group students flexibly for guided reading instruction?

3 Describe some ways to help struggling readers when using reciprocal teaching during guided reading instruction.

4 What are some ways to manage the class while working with guided reading groups?

5 What are some ways to prompt individual students to use reciprocal teaching strategies during guided reading instruction?

6 What other comprehension strategies are important to scaffold during guided reading groups?

7 How can comprehension charts help guide and record reciprocal teaching discussions? Give some examples of the use of charts with fiction and nonfiction texts.

8 How can you teach students to retell and summarize?

9 Discuss with students ways to assess their use of reciprocal teaching strategies during guided reading instruction.

CHAPTER 4

RECIPROCAL TEACHING

in Literature Circles

Summarize is when you tell in two or three sentences what happened in the book. Sometimes it's hard, especially if there is a part you need to clarify. Summarizing helps me remember what I read.

—Rachael, grade 4

Description of Reciprocal Teaching and Literature Circles

The sixth graders at Palmecia School in Hayward, California, look forward to their weekly literature circles when they take on the reciprocal teaching roles of predictor, questioner, clarifier, summarizer, and discussion director in literature circles. They meet to discuss reading materials that range from a chapter in their social studies textbook to a novel. The result is a series of lively exchanges that improves their reading comprehension.

According to Vygotsky (1934/1978), learning is social and students use language and discussions to construct negotiated understandings. The cooperative nature and scaffolded support of reciprocal teaching make it a natural match for student-led discussion circles. A literature circle provides a unique environment for boosting comprehension with reciprocal teaching strategies because it is a natural setting in which students can take turns using each reciprocal teaching strategy—predicting, questioning, clarifying, and summarizing. In addition, reciprocal teaching can be incorporated easily into a literature circle format at a variety of grade levels. Just ask the sixth graders at Palmecia School in Haywood, California, and the second and third graders at Del Rey in Orinda, California: They will tell you that the combination of reciprocal teaching and literature circles improves reading comprehension and, most of all, is fun.

Using reciprocal teaching during literature circles strengthens students' reading comprehension by offering

- more opportunities to participate and time for guided practice in each reciprocal teaching strategy;
- a highly participatory, small-group format;
- the opportunity to work through content area reading material in a cooperative group;
- the support of a peer group for scaffolding of the reciprocal teaching strategies;
- the chance to form groups based on student choice; and
- opportunities for students to become more metacognitive and independent in their use of reciprocal teaching strategies.

It was out of necessity that I finally developed a model for reciprocal teaching in literature circles. I had been meeting with a group of six struggling fourth graders twice a week for reciprocal teaching sessions. The group worked hard, and, after three months of guided reading lessons with reciprocal teaching, most of them had improved one year in their reading levels. Then, their classroom teacher decided that the students could not miss any more regular class time for the intervention sessions. Although I understood her frustration, I desperately wanted to find a way to continue helping the students hone their use of reciprocal teaching strategies. It was then that I asked the struggling students to be my experts and help me to introduce reciprocal teaching strategies to their entire class. Beaming with pride at their accomplishments, they gladly assisted me in modeling for the class and in leading the literature circles. By the end of the school year, all of the struggling students had raised their reading levels, comprehension abilities, self-esteem, and motivation to read.

For those teachers who like the structure of official roles (Daniels, 1994) in literature circles, the reciprocal teaching roles of predictor, questioner, clarifier, and summarizer work well. I add a fifth role—a discussion director—to assist with additional, essential reading comprehension strategies such as making connections and visualizing to improve comprehension, and with tasks such as filling in graphic organizers.

If you do not want to use reciprocal teaching roles, then another option is to allow your students to discuss the strategies freely. Then, one student can record the group's collective predictions, questions, points or words to clarify, and summary (Routman, 1999). Roles or no roles, I hold every student responsible for knowing how to use all the reciprocal teaching strategies when reading a given text. I often do this by calling on students from each of the literature circles at random to give examples of the strategies.

Goals of Reciprocal Teaching During Literature Circles

The goals of reciprocal teaching during literature circles are

- to deepen comprehension using a peer collaborative setting and reciprocal teaching strategies,
- to provide opportunities for students to practice the four reciprocal teaching strategies,
- to enhance reading comprehension in nonfiction or fiction texts, and
- to guide students in becoming metacognitive and independent in their use of reciprocal teaching strategies.

Reciprocal teaching adds a "read and learn to comprehend" dimension to literature circles because it gives students the basics for comprehending texts well. I decided to try using reciprocal teaching strategies in literature circles because many students with whom I worked were reading and not comprehending what they were reading. I knew research indicated that gains could be made with reciprocal teaching strategies even when peers interact (Palincsar, Brown, & Martin, 1987), and literature circles provide more opportunities for scaffolding reading strategies. More teachers are starting to incorporate reciprocal teaching into their literature circles, which may already include other wonderful models and variations that promote discussion (Daniels, 1994; Hill, Johnson, & Noe, 1995; Samway & Wang, 1995).

An added benefit of using reciprocal teaching in literature circles is that the reciprocal teaching model teaches and reinforces basic reading comprehension strategies. Some primary teachers with whom I work prefer reciprocal teaching during literature circles because their students are still learning to read and reciprocal teaching is easy to implement with primary students. Teachers are attracted to students' growth in the four fundamental strategies and four basic reciprocal teaching strategies that become tasks during the literature circle model. Some teachers gradually introduce reciprocal teaching during guided reading groups and whole-class sessions over the school year as part of their plan to teach students to read. By the spring, their students are capable of participating fully in reciprocal teaching during literature circles.

Organizing Literature Circles in Your Classroom

In order to provide a rich reciprocal teaching experience for all students, I usually opt for creating literature circles that are heterogeneous. If I have met regularly with struggling students to use reciprocal teaching strategies with them, when I begin working with the whole class I invite the struggling students to be the experts. I include one of them in each literature circle. This way, the struggling readers have the opportunity to shine as they train the heterogeneous groups to use reciprocal teaching strategies.

In addition to organizing heterogeneous literature circles, I also like to give students opportunities to form groups based on their shared interest in a particular text. I offer several different books for students to choose from, and they form groups based on their book choices. To ensure that the books are not too challenging or easy for some students, I offer a variety of texts but try to keep the material at the students' grade level.

What books work best for reciprocal teaching literature circles? When first introducing a class to reciprocal teaching in literature circles, use short, easy-to-read, high-interest books and articles. During the introductory phase, you do not want the students to become bogged down with material that is too difficult to read and understand. However, once the students know the reciprocal teaching routine and strategies, you can switch to textbook and novel chapters and the school district's grade-level anthology. Struggling students can read with a group member as a partner, or you can assist students who need extra support in the actual reading of the material.

In order for any literature circle model to flow smoothly, you should train your students in reciprocal teaching strategies, social skills, and other necessary procedures. Figure 22 outlines the training that students need and some basic ways to conduct it. Many of these fundamentals are incorporated into the lessons in this chapter. (See Figure 23 for an overview of the lessons presented in this chapter.)

The Big Picture in Literature Circles: What Else You Will Need to Do

Although I highly recommend reciprocal teaching strategies for use in literature circles, I have reservations about exclusively using reciprocal teaching strategies in this setting. I try to consider and incorporate other important strategies that promote reading comprehension, such as making connections and inferences and discussing a text's theme (McLaughlin & Allen, 2002). You also may want to continue using other literature circle models (Daniels, 1994; Hill et al., 1995; Samway & Wang, 1995) to ensure that your students have the opportunity to work collaboratively with a variety of essential reading strategies. See Figure 24 on page 138 for other books that discuss literature circles.

Reciprocal teaching in literature circles can provide students with an extra boost toward improving the basic reading comprehension strategies that all good readers use. Because I also continue to value the strategies covered by other literature circle models in addition to my reciprocal teaching model, I have developed a variety of plans for literature circle implementation. In this way, students learn from reciprocal teaching and

Figure 22
Training for Reciprocal Teaching in Literature Circles

Training That Students Need Prior to Literature Circles	Why?	How to Model and Teach
Training in reciprocal teaching strategies—predict, question, clarify, and summarize	• Students need a deep understanding of all four strategies so they can participate fully in discussions. • Each student needs to be ready to give a response for each strategy.	• Model and guide through reciprocal teaching strategies during whole-class lessons with partners, during guided reading lessons with small groups, and when using role sheets during guided reading as a training ground for literature circles.
Training in social skills—taking turns, being polite, practicing active listening skills, and building on others' comments	• Literature circles will not run smoothly without the necessary social skills. • Students can learn a lot from their peers, but social skills must first be modeled, taught, and reinforced.	• Ask one group to model social skills for the class. Choose model groups often. • Have the class respond to the model group by discussing the Reciprocal Teaching Observation Chart (page 100).
Training in necessary procedures—minilessons on how to use materials and act out roles, filling out graphic organizers, and completing other response activities	• Students need to know basic procedures in order to function effectively within literature circles. • Students should know the routines associated with literature circles to allow them to focus on what they are reading.	• Discuss and model minilessons on procedures for materials, roles, and responses. • Model these activities with one group in front of the class. • Practice and/or guide students in these procedures during guided reading sessions with one group at a time.

also have the opportunity to benefit from the more open-ended, aesthetic responses that other models promote (see, for example, Daniels, 1994; Hill et al., 1995).

In some classrooms, I use reciprocal teaching exclusively with certain texts and reserve other literature circle models for use with other designated texts. For example, a sixth-grade teacher with whom I work was concerned because she had already taught her students to use

Figure 23
Lesson Overview Chart: Reciprocal Teaching in Literature Circles

Lesson	Pages	Description
Introducing Reciprocal Teaching in Literature Circles	143 to 157	A student group models reciprocal teaching literature circles for the class.
Using Role Sheets During Reciprocal Teaching in Literature Circles	158 to 165	Role sheets are used for each of the five roles.
Using What I Know and What I Wonder Strips	166 to 169	Students write what they know and wonder about on strips for a group chart prior to reading.
Practicing Reciprocal Teaching Strategies With the Reciprocal Teaching Spinner	169 to 172	Using the Reciprocal Teaching Spinner, students spin and land on a reciprocal teaching strategy that they must demonstrate.
Organizing Cross-Age Buddy Sessions With Reciprocal Teaching	173 to 178	Cross-age buddies work together using the four reciprocal teaching strategies as they read.
Minilesson: I Predict That I Will Learn…	179	Students predict with a nonfiction text.
Minilesson: Question, Answer, and Pass	180	Students generate questions on cards and play a passing game.
Minilesson: Concentrate on Clarifying	181	Students write words to clarify and their respective clarification strategies on index cards and play a concentration game.
Minilesson: A "Clear" Summary	182	Groups work to construct summaries on overhead transparencies.

Daniels's (1994) literature circle roles of discussion director, passage picker, summarizer, artful artist, word finder, and connector. She felt that it would be confusing to introduce her students to another set of jobs in order to use reciprocal teaching in literature circles. I suggested that she might want to use Daniels's model with fiction and the reciprocal teaching model with nonfiction, including textbooks. This idea may be limiting because reciprocal teaching works well with fiction and nonfiction. However, if you prefer to continue implementing a literature circle model that you already find successful, then try reserving certain texts for the reciprocal teaching model.

Another way to include strategies that fall outside reciprocal teaching in literature circles is to incorporate the special role of discussion director. When I first designed the reciprocal teaching-

Figure 24
Books on Literature Circles

Daniels, H. (1994). *Literature circles: Voice and choice in the student-centered classroom.* York, ME: Stenhouse.

Daniels, H. (2001). *Literature circles: Voice and choice in book clubs and reading groups.* York, ME: Stenhouse.

Flint, A.S. (1999). *Literature circles: A professional's guide.* Westminster, CA: Teacher Created Materials.

Hill, B.C., Johnson, N.J., & Noe, K.S. (1995). *Literature circles and response.* Norwood, MA: Christopher-Gordon.

Hill, B.C., Johnson, N.J., & Noe, K.S. (2000). *Literature circles resource guide: Teaching suggestions, forms, sample booklists, and database.* Norwood, MA: Christopher-Gordon.

Marriott, D. (2002). *Comprehension right from the start: How to organize and manage book clubs for young readers.* Portsmouth, NH: Heinemann.

Samway, K.D., & Wang, G. (1995). *Literature study circles in a multicultural classroom.* York, ME: Stenhouse.

Vasquez, V. (with Muise, M.R., Adamson, S.C., Heffernan, L., Chiola-Nakai, D., & Shear, J.). (2003). *Getting beyond "I like the book": Creating space for critical literacy in K–6 classrooms.* Newark, DE: International Reading Association.

literature circle model complete with role sheets (pages 151–154), I had only four basic roles—a predictor, questioner, clarifier, and summarizer. As the students began working their way through the strategies, I found that something was missing. My literature circle model limited students by omitting some important reading strategies. I felt the need to have students discuss what they already knew about a topic and what they wondered about it before reading a nonfiction text. When they were engaged in fiction, I wanted students to make connections between the text and their own lives and discuss open-ended responses. The reciprocal teaching roles were simply not enough to encompass all of the discussion points that I wanted students to share.

I decided to include a literature discussion director who would play a sort of catchall role for reading strategies and social skills. The discussion director involves the students in other important reading comprehension strategies that good readers should use. Because fiction and nonfiction require slightly different responses and strategies, I designed two role sheets for the discussion director that include reading strategies and social skills necessary for working with these text types (pages 155–156). The discussion director also may lead the group in creating a graphic organizer or an artistic response to the reading. After the first time that I used the discussion director role, the reciprocal teaching literature circles worked much more smoothly, and I felt reassured that I was including other important reading comprehension strategies in my lessons.

Assessment Options for Reciprocal Teaching in Literature Circles

Assessment of students' achievements during literature circles can be approached from a variety of angles. Sometimes I require students to produce a group product such as a written response for all four reciprocal teaching strategies, and on other occasions I ask individual students to turn in a written piece. Students need to know that they should be ready at all times because anytime you might call on them to share their knowledge with the group.

The following assessment opportunities can be used alone or in combination to provide important data to inform your instruction in reciprocal teaching strategies and literature circle procedures:

- Circulate around the classroom and observe your students during reciprocal teaching literature circles. Take notes on how your students are performing each strategy in the groups (use the rubric in Appendix A on page 195 as a guide). Also, make notes regarding your students' social skills. Observe whether they take turns, ask for clarification, signal agreement, and use other group-process skills. As needed, teach the minilessons for literature circles found on pages 179–182.

- During your observations, choose a group that is doing well with all four strategies. After the literature circle session is over, invite the whole class to surround the group that you have selected. Have the chosen group model reading a page of text and working through reciprocal teaching strategies. Invite the class to respond to and evaluate the group's modeling in addition to making note of the social skills that the group models. If time constraints do not allow for the group members to model the strategies at the end of the literature circle session, then ask them to model the strategies at the beginning of the next session.

- Hold all groups accountable for the work that they do during reciprocal teaching in literature circles. Tell the groups that they each must choose a group member to record their reciprocal teaching responses on the Literature Discussion Sheet for Reciprocal Teaching (see sheet on page 141). The group also can prepare a "clear" summary (see minilesson on page 182) on a transparency for the overhead projector.

- Hold individual students accountable for their work during reciprocal teaching literature circles. Rather than asking a group to turn in one Literature Discussion Sheet for Reciprocal Teaching, you can require that every student turn in a copy of the form. Or, you can simply have each student write a response to the four strategies on a sheet of paper. Hold students verbally accountable for their learning, too. Let them know that you may call on them anytime and they must have responses ready when you do.

- Observe all the groups and join one group for a few minutes while group members discuss reciprocal teaching strategies. Coach, model, and praise the students in the group as needed. Instead of presenting minilessons (pages 179–182) to the whole class, work with each group to guide the members through the necessary reinforcement. Also, be prepared to coach a group in any reciprocal teaching strategy with which it is having difficulty. Use Figure 4 on page 21 when students are struggling.

- Invite students to use the Self-Assessment Form for Reciprocal Teaching Literature Circles (see form on page 142) to evaluate their own progress with the use of reciprocal teaching strategies. Have the discussion leaders share with the class how the group did. Model the strategies based on difficulties that show up in the evaluations and coach each group as needed.

- Provide the whole class with additional modeling of and practice with reciprocal teaching strategies by using the minilessons on pages 179–182 before breaking into reciprocal teaching literature circles. Reteach the minilessons to individuals and groups of students who are struggling with particular strategies.

Literature Discussion Sheet for Reciprocal Teaching

Group Members: _____

Predict	**Question**
Fiction	Here are questions I can ask my group (who, what, when, where, why, how, what if):
I predict that _____	
_____	1. _____
_____	_____
_____	_____
because _____	_____
_____	2. _____
_____	_____
Nonfiction	_____
I think I will learn	_____
_____	3. _____
_____	_____
because _____	_____
_____	_____
_____	_____

Clarify	**Summarize**
1. _____ is a difficult word because	Here is a one- or two-sentence summary:
_____.	_____
So I (check the strategies that you used)	_____
__ checked parts of the word that I know.	_____
__ sounded out the word.	_____
__ thought of a word that looks like this.	_____
__ read on to find clues.	_____
__ reread to find clues.	_____
__ tried another word.	_____
	_____
2. _____ is a confusing idea because	_____
_____.	_____
So I (check the strategies that you used)	_____
__ reread.	_____
__ read on.	_____
__ thought about what I know.	_____
__ talked to a friend.	_____

Self-Assessment Form for Reciprocal Teaching Literature Circles

1. I participated in the discussion

____a lot   ____ some   ____ a little   ____ not at all

2. I listened to others in the group

____ a lot   ____ some   ____ a little   ____ not at all

3. I looked at others when they were talking

____ a lot   ____ some   ____ a little   ____ not at all

4. I gave answers for all four reciprocal teaching strategies.

Predict   __ yes   __ no

Question   __ yes   __ no

Clarify   __ yes   __ no

Summarize   __ yes   __ no

5. Here is a drawing of what I did best today.

6. Here is a drawing and writing to describe what I could do next time to improve.

Lesson 1: Introducing Reciprocal Teaching in Literature Circles

 Predict   **Question**   **Clarify**   **Summarize**

Reciprocal Teaching Strategies in This Lesson

Background and Description

When it is literature circle time in Mrs. Garcia's fifth-grade classroom, her students sit in circles of five on the classroom floor, huddled over their books. While one group's members ask one another questions after reading a text and another group acts out a chapter summary, Mrs. Garcia might meet with a third group to listen in and guide the students as they discuss ideas and words to clarify. Her literature circles run smoothly because she has provided her students with ample support in reciprocal teaching in a variety of ways before introducing them to reciprocal teaching in literature circles. For example, she taught whole-class and guided reading lessons to model the reciprocal teaching strategies with both fiction and nonfiction texts. When she introduced reciprocal teaching literature circles to her class, she asked for volunteers to model the strategies for the class, and she has done so every day since then. Mrs. Garcia's literature circles did not come together in just a few lessons; she carefully introduced them with a lot of support. You will need to do the same for your students.

This lesson will give you some ideas for introducing reciprocal teaching literature circles to your class. How do you know whether your students are ready for literature circles that involve reciprocal teaching strategies? Students who are ready for working with reciprocal teaching in these groups need to be very familiar with each reciprocal teaching strategy and trained in the social skills that are necessary for polite and meaningful exchanges with their peers. The lesson requires student evaluations of a peer group's use of reciprocal teaching strategies and social skills and student participation as rotating leaders for each reciprocal teaching strategy.

A reciprocal teaching literature circle needs a discussion director to lead other group members in additional reading comprehension strategies, such as building background knowledge; making connections; and discussing feelings, the author's craft, and character motives (Keene

& Zimmermann, 1997; McLaughlin & Allen, 2002; Pearson et al., 1992). In addition, you will need to train your students in the social skills necessary for participation in literature circles, and use other kinds of literature circles with your students (Daniels, 1994; Hill et al., 1995; Samway & Wang, 1995). (The Classroom Story on page 147 offers an example of a successful literature circle session using reciprocal teaching strategies.)

Materials

- A copy of the Be the Teacher Bookmark (page 53) for each student
- Role sheets duplicated for each reciprocal teaching role (see role sheets on pages 151–154, and 155 or 156)
- Pieces of tagboard folded in half lengthwise, with a role sheet glued on one side and the appropriate role title—predictor, questioner, clarifier, summarizer, discussion director—written on the other side (place these labels in front of the appropriate student in the literature circle so the group will remember which role each student is playing)
- A copy of the Reciprocal Teaching Observation Sheet (see sheet on page 157) for each student
- A copy of Using the Reciprocal Teaching Team When I Read (see Appendix B on page 202) for each student.
- A chart or whiteboard to record discussion points
- A copy of the reading material for each student

Teacher Modeling

Prior to this lesson, all your students should be proficient in the four reciprocal teaching strategies. They should have learned the strategies in either guided reading groups or whole-class lessons.

1. Introduce reciprocal teaching in literature circles by telling your students that they are going to see what a literature circle using reciprocal teaching strategies looks like. Tell them that they will have the opportunity to be responsible for either one of the strategies or the discussion director role.

2. Review reciprocal teaching strategies via a class discussion or by modeling each strategy for your students. Give each student a Be the Teacher Bookmark (page 53) for reference.

3. Select a group of students to model a literature circle using reciprocal teaching strategies.

   Have the students in the group display signs indicating which role they are playing—predictor, questioner, clarifier, summarizer, or discussion director (see Figure 25).

4. Ask each student in the model group to perform his or her role and walk the group members through a reciprocal teaching discussion in front of the class.

Student Participation

1. Give each student a copy of the Reciprocal Teaching Observation Sheet (page 157) so students can keep track of what the model group does well and what they need to improve. The observers either can stand in a circle around the table where the model group is working or sit at their desks while the model group sits in front of the class.

2. Begin with the discussion director, and instruct him or her to ask the students in the model group to introduce themselves and their roles. The discussion director should ask the predictor to go first.

Figure 25
Students Participate in a Literature Circle With Role Sheets

3. The predictor asks the group to preview the illustrations, headings, and covers of the chosen text. Then, he or she asks the group members to think of a prediction. The predictor can give a prediction first before prompting the other group members for their predictions.

4. Next, the discussion director either selects a mode of reading or asks the model group how it wants to read the selected pages—silently, aloud in pairs, or aloud by pages or paragraphs. The group begins reading in its chosen manner.

   The students in the rest of the class should have copies of the text and should read at the same time so they can follow the discussion.

5. After reading, the discussion director asks the model group members who would like to go next—the questioner, clarifier, or summarizer. Each student who has a role takes a turn and performs his or her role before asking the rest of the group to follow suit (that is, the questioner asks a question first, then asks others to do so).

   The discussion director should compliment participation and good strategy use. The group should end with the predictor predicting what will happen in the next segment of the text.

6. Ask the class to give the group compliments and suggestions regarding both strategy use and proper literature circle etiquette. The discussion director may call on students from the observer group to give the feedback.

   Using the behaviors listed on the Reciprocal Teaching Observation Sheet (page 157), guide the class to create a rubric for literature circle etiquette. Make a two-column chart together that outlines what a literature circle should look and sound like. Students may add other behaviors not listed on the observation sheet. Refer to the class-created chart often when reinforcing proper behavior for literature circles.

7. Have students help you review the use of the four strategies in a literature circle. Pass out copies of Using the Reciprocal Teaching Team When I Read (see Appendix B, page 202) and review together the guidelines for each strategy. Ask students to remember these

important steps for each strategy as they participate in literature circles and take on roles.

8. In another session, or on the same day if there is time, try the suggestions in Lesson 2 on page 158 to guide the class in using reciprocal teaching literature circles on their own.

- Observe your students in their literature circles, and take notes so you can group students who are having trouble with a particular strategy for a quick minilesson on that strategy. See the minilessons on pages 179–182.

- Some forms in this book (for example, the Literature Discussion Sheet for Reciprocal Teaching on page 141) can be used for written assessments. Students may fill out the chosen form either as a group or individuals. After you review the forms, group students according to the strategy with which they need the most help. Teach the minilessons on pages 179–182 to the groups who need support.

- Continue modeling with one student group in front of the class so students can discuss the strategies and social skills necessary for an effective reciprocal teaching literature circle.

Introducing Literature Circles to Grades 2–3 With Role Sheets

The second and third graders in Mrs. Brown's classroom are studying habitats, and I have decided to bring in four different nonfiction books about habitats from which the students can choose. The Exploring Habitats series works well for reciprocal teaching circles because each book has interesting but simple text with great nonfiction features such as a table of contents, headings, a glossary, and an index. The short, four-page chapters are convenient to use in separate reciprocal teaching sessions because students can read a manageable chunk of text and then discuss reciprocal teaching strategies. I use both the Big Books and accompanying little books for all four titles in the series—*Exploring Freshwater Habitats* (Snowball, 1995), *Exploring Saltwater Habitats* (Smith, 1994), *Exploring Land Habitats* (Phinney, 1995), and *Exploring Tree Habitats* (Seifert, 1995).

The students already are familiar with reciprocal teaching strategies because Mrs. Brown and I taught them the strategies in guided reading and whole-class lessons for several months. Although the students have not worked in literature circles before, we conduct our guided reading lessons in such a way that the students are able to practice the necessary strategies and social skills to prepare them to work independently.

I begin today's lesson by giving a short talk about each book choice. Then, I place the books on the chalkboard tray and ask the students to write their first and second choices on a slip of paper. During recess, I look over the students' choices and arrange groups of five students who will read the same book. When the students return to the classroom, they listen eagerly as I call out their names. I ask each student to come up to the front of the room and sit quietly in one of four areas where I have the groups' assigned books displayed.

Then, I select the group using the book on freshwater habitats to be the model group for the class. I pass out the reciprocal teaching role sheets, which the students have used with my assistance during previous guided reading groups. The model group works through the first chapter of their book in front of the class, using the reciprocal teaching roles.

Before Reading: Activating Background Knowledge and Making Predictions for the Entire Book   I allow the five group members in the model group to select their respective reciprocal teaching literature circle roles. Sam, an outgoing and very verbal child, is designated as the discussion director. He begins by giving each group member two 1-inch-wide and 8-inch-long strips of construction paper—one yellow and one green.

Sam checks his role sheet to read the directions before he begins. Then, he boldly requests of his group, "Please take the green strip and write on it one thing that you know about freshwater habitats. You can look at the book's cover to help you remember what you know." The other group members study the cover and begin to jot down responses such as "I know that freshwater doesn't have salt in it," "I know that turtles and snails live in freshwater habitats," and "I know that a river is a freshwater habitat."

After they all finish, Sam takes a large piece of construction paper and writes on it the heading "What We Know About Freshwater Habitats." He passes a roll of tape around the group, and each student tapes his or her strip under the heading. Then, each student reads aloud his or her What I Know strip to the group.

Next, Sam asks the group members to look at the book's table of contents. He calls on Anthony to read the chapter titles, which are "Rivers," "Marshes," "Lakes," "Streams," "Cypress Swamps," "Glossary," and "Index." Then, Sam asks the group to look through the pictures in the book for a minute or two. "But, no reading, guys! Only read the headings and labels!" he requests.

After the group members finish reading, Sam invites them to think about what they wonder about freshwater habitats based on what they saw in the illustrations and asks them each to write on the yellow strip of construction paper something that they wonder. The students hunch over their strips and fervently write what they wonder.

Sam quickly writes "What We Wonder" on the bottom half of the large sheet of construction paper, leaving room for the wonder strips to be attached below the heading. Once again, Sam asks the group to share their responses before taping them to the poster, and they read "I wonder what kinds of animals live in river habitats," "I wonder what the food chain looks like in a marsh," and "I wonder what animals live near lakes."

Next, Sam politely asks the predictor, Anthony, to take on his role. Anthony fumbles a bit but refers to his role sheet for guidance. Then, he asks the group to look at the illustrations, headings, and labels in the chapter titled "Rivers." He calls on volunteers to discuss what they see on the pages.

Anthony passes out copies of the Literature Discussion Sheet for Reciprocal Teaching to all the students and tells them to fill in one thing that they think they will learn.

The students write the following predictions:

"I think I will learn about birds that live on the river. I will learn about the kingfisher and flamingo, and shoe-billed stork."

"I think I will learn about crocodiles on the river and what they eat."

"I will learn how the food chain works on a river."

During Reading: Choosing a Mode of Reading   Anthony asks for a show of hands from students who have ideas for how to read the text. Rebecca thinks that they should take turns reading with partners and that because Sam will not have a partner, he can help the pairs if they get stuck. Sam agrees, and he silently reads the material while the two pairs alternate reading aloud.

After Reading: Questioning, Summarizing, and Clarifying   After reading, Sam asks who would like to go next—the questioner, clarifier, or summarizer. Rebecca, the questioner, offers to take her turn. She asks the group members each to write a question on their discussion forms. Then, they each take turns asking their questions and calling on group members to answer. Anthony asks, "What are four animals in the food chain on the Nile River?" Three students raise their hands, and he calls on Rebecca to answer. She responds with only two animals from the text, the larva and the frog, and says that she does not remember any others. Because we have practiced answering one another's questions in guided reading groups, Anthony knows how to prompt her to answer correctly. He asks Rebecca to reread page 6. After rereading, Rebecca adds the Nile monitor and the Nile crocodile to her response, and Anthony compliments her with a resounding, "Good job."

Then, Sam calls on the clarifier, Julio, to take his turn leading the group through the process of selecting a difficult word and explaining how to clarify it. Julio chooses to clarify the word *depends* because he had trouble reading it. He tells the students that he knew the prefix *de* and the last chunk *pends*, so he combined them to make *depends*. Julio also explains how he read the sentence and that word made sense. Next, Julio calls on each group member to select a word and share how he or she figured it out.

In an effort to move the group along, Sam calls on the summarizer, Angela. I interrupt to tell Angela that she may want to have the group members work in pairs to summarize aloud before they write summaries on their discussion sheets. She agrees, and after the students do just that, Angela shares her summary: "These pages are about a certain river habitat, the Nile River. Many plants and animals live on the Nile," she concludes reluctantly.

The other students each share their summaries. I interrupt to ask the class to tell me whether details such as the hippo's weight or the length of a Nile perch fish are important to include in a summary. The class agrees that while the facts are interesting, they are details and do not belong in a summary. I am pleased that the students have come so far with summarizing.

Sam closes the discussion by asking the group members if they have any other comments. No one responds, so he compliments them for their strategy use and their efforts to coach one another when they were stuck. He asks the group what they need to work on next. Angela suggests that the students not interrupt one another. I ask the class to talk in pairs to discuss what compliments and suggestions they have for the model reciprocal teaching group. After the pairs convene, I lead a whole-class discussion on the topic. The students are very complimentary to the group, remarking, "You had good predictions based on clues," "You took turns," and "You guys were nice to each other."

I ask the class if they all would like to start working in their groups the next day, and I receive a resounding "Yes." After this in-depth modeling session and the previous reciprocal teaching lessons that Mrs. Brown and I have taught in whole-class and guided reading sessions, these students are ready for literature circles.

Reflection and Next Steps   During the next week or so, the students will meet with their literature circles to work through the habitat texts. Before each group meets, we will review the four reciprocal teaching strategies and the literature circle procedures. After each literature circle session, I will have one circle serve as the model group, and I will invite the group members' classmates to observe them and comment on their use of the strategies.

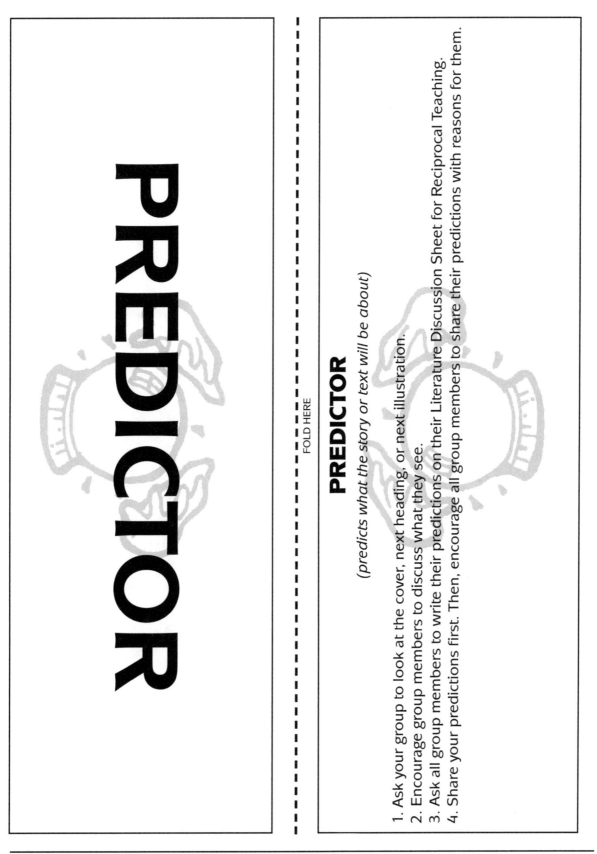

PREDICTOR

PREDICTOR

(predicts what the story or text will be about)

1. Ask your group to look at the cover, next heading, or next illustration.
2. Encourage group members to discuss what they see.
3. Ask all group members to write their predictions on their Literature Discussion Sheet for Reciprocal Teaching.
4. Share your predictions first. Then, encourage all group members to share their predictions with reasons for them.

FOLD HERE

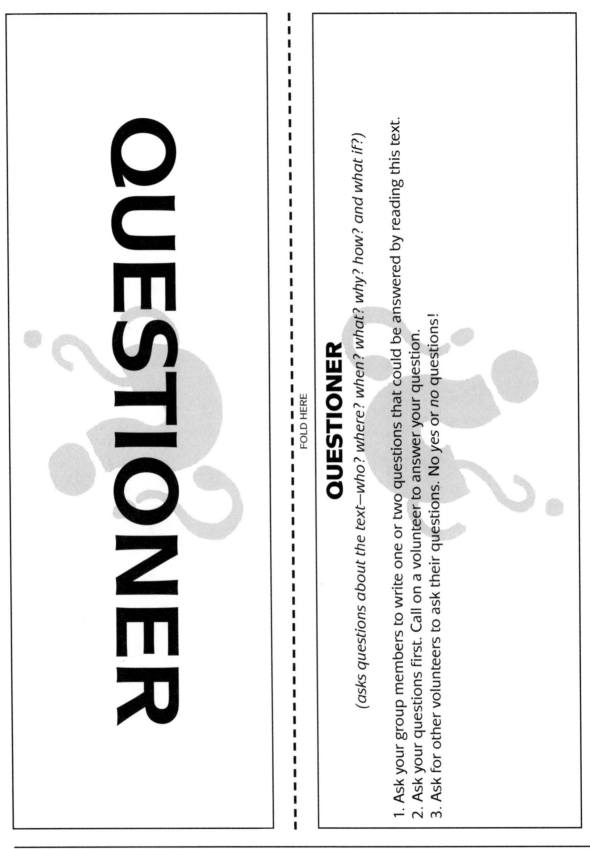

QUESTIONER

QUESTIONER

(asks questions about the text—who? where? when? what? why? how? and what if?)

1. Ask your group members to write one or two questions that could be answered by reading this text.
2. Ask your questions first. Call on a volunteer to answer your question.
3. Ask for other volunteers to ask their questions. No *yes* or *no* questions!

FOLD HERE

CLARIFIER

FOLD HERE

CLARIFIER

(finds areas where a word or idea needs to be explained—reread, read ahead, use what you know, break a word into chunks, and think about what makes sense)

1. Ask the group to reread this portion of text and look for confusing ideas or words. (What if you had to explain the book to a kindergartner?)

2. Ask the group to write one confusing or difficult word or idea.

3. Share your word or idea first. Tell how you figured it out, using the Clarifying Bookmarks.

4. Ask for volunteers to give their words and ideas. Ask how they figured them out. If someone has a difficult word or idea that he or she didn't figure out, ask group members for ways to clarify the unclear word or idea.

Reciprocal Teaching at Work: Strategies for Improving Reading Comprehension by Lori D. Oczkus © 2003.
Newark, DE: International Reading Association. May be copied for classroom use.

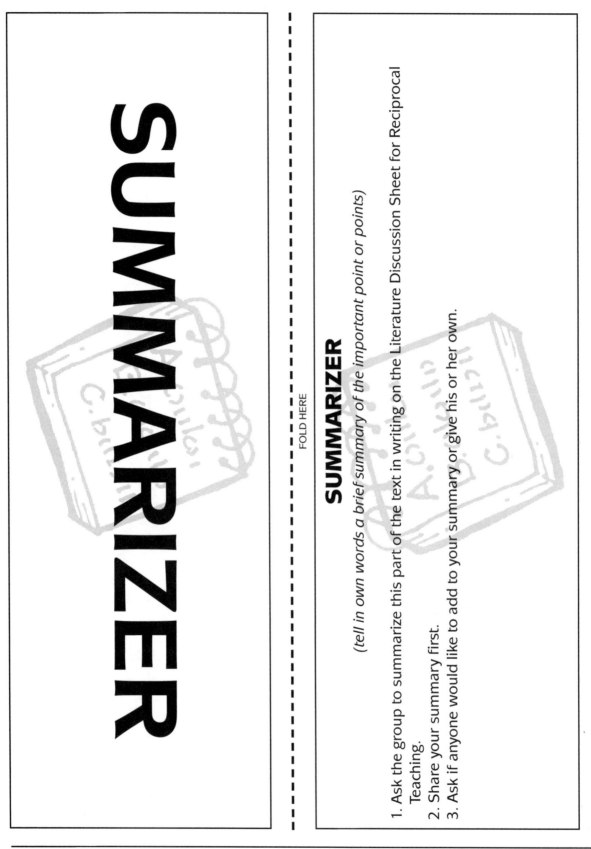

SUMMARIZER

FOLD HERE

SUMMARIZER

(tell in own words a brief summary of the important point or points)

1. Ask the group to summarize this part of the text in writing on the Literature Discussion Sheet for Reciprocal Teaching.

2. Share your summary first.

3. Ask if anyone would like to add to your summary or give his or her own.

DISCUSSION DIRECTOR ROLE SHEET FOR FICTION

DISCUSSION DIRECTOR ROLE SHEET FOR FICTION

The discussion director keeps the discussion going, fills in the comprehension chart, and helps the group evaluate its performance.

Before Reading

1. Ask the predictor to go first.
2. After the predictor's turn, decide how the group will read the text—aloud, silently, or in pairs.

After Reading

1. Ask who would like to go first—the questioner, clarifier, or summarizer. Keep the discussion going. If the group did not finish reading the book, the predictor can take another turn to ask, What will happen next?

2. Ask each group member to share his or her connection strips for text-to-self, text-to-text, and text-to-world connections. Glue the connections to a chart.

3. Compliment the group for their behavior and use of reciprocal teaching strategies. Invite the group members to compliment one another: "Good eye contact," "Great idea," or "Good turn-taking."

FOLD HERE

DISCUSSION DIRECTOR ROLE SHEET FOR NONFICTION

FOLD HERE

DISCUSSION DIRECTOR ROLE SHEET FOR NONFICTION

The discussion director keeps the discussion going, fills in the What I Know and What I Wonder Chart, and helps the group evaluate its performance.

Before Reading

1. Ask everyone to share his or her I Know strips.
2. Ask everyone to share his or her I Wonder strips. Glue the strips to the What I Know and What I Wonder chart.
3. Ask the predictor to take a turn making predictions.
4. After the predictor's turn, decide how the group will read the text—aloud, silently, or in pairs.

After Reading

1. Ask who would like to go first—the questioner, clarifier, or summarizer. Keep the discussion going.
2. Return to the I Wonder strips. Ask if anyone had his or her question answered in the reading. Ask if there are any new questions.
3. Compliment the group members for their behavior and use of reciprocal teaching strategies. Invite the group members to compliment one another: "Good eye contact," "Great idea," or "Good turn-taking."

Reciprocal Teaching Observation Sheet

Observer's Name:

Group Members' Names:

Looks Like	Sounds Like
What does the model group look like?	**What does the model group sound like?**
(Check all that apply.)	(Check all that apply.)
___ They sat still. (no fidgeting)	___ They were polite to one another.
___ They looked at each other when talking. (nodded heads, smiled)	___ They were nice when they disagreed. ("I see what you mean, but I think….")
___ They looked back at the book.	___ They stayed on topic.
	___ They piggybacked on one another's comments. ("I agree. I want to add….")
	___ They didn't interrupt one another.
	___ They helped one another.
	___ They praised one another. ("Good job," "Nice prediction," and so on.)
	___ Everyone participated in the discussion.
Compliment	**Compliment**
What is one compliment that you could give the model group?	What is one compliment that you could give the model group?
Improvement	**Improvement**
How could the group improve the way that they look when they work together?	How could the group improve the way that they sound?

Lesson 2: Using Role Sheets During Reciprocal Teaching in Literature Circles

Predict **Question** **Clarify** **Summarize**

Background and Description

When I first began using reciprocal teaching strategies in literature circles, I eventually felt the need to create role sheets for each role. Without role sheets, I found that many groups raced through the four roles and, after only a few minutes of discussion, proudly raised their hands, announcing, "We're done, Mrs. Oczkus!" The role sheets that I designed for each reciprocal teaching strategy role guide students in their jobs. I have been pleased with the results: The students use the role sheets to stay focused and on task (see this lesson in action with struggling readers in the Classroom Story on page 162). As an option, you can have your students rotate roles within the group so each student gets a chance to play each role and use each role sheet.

In situations in which the students become especially proficient in reciprocal teaching strategies, you eventually can set aside the role sheets and continue the reciprocal teaching discussions in a less structured fashion. It is up to you to decide just how much you want your students to rely on the role sheets during reciprocal teaching literature circles.

In this lesson, there are suggestions for further modeling (see Lesson 1 on page 143) with a student group and ideas for guiding students as you prepare them to work on their own in literature circles. Train your students in other aspects of literature circles covered by the discussion director, including discussing background knowledge, asking questions before reading, making connections, and using proper social skills (Keene & Zimmermann, 1997; McLaughlin & Allen, 2002; Pearson et al., 1992).

Materials

- Multiple copies of reading material for both the reciprocal teaching model group and the observers
- Role sheets duplicated for each reciprocal teaching group of five students (pages 151–154, and 155 or 156)

- Pieces of tagboard folded in half lengthwise, with a role sheet glued on one side and the appropriate role title—predictor, questioner, clarifier, summarizer, discussion director (for fiction or nonfiction, depending on the text)—written on the other side (place these labels in front of the appropriate student in the model group so the group will remember which role each student is playing)
- A copy of the Reciprocal Teaching Observation Sheet (page 157) for each student
- A copy of the What We Know and What We Wonder Chart (page 164) for each student
- Optional: copies of the Literature Discussion Sheet for Reciprocal Teaching (page 141)—one per group or student for recording discussions

Teacher Modeling

1. In this lesson, guide a new model group (see Lesson 1 on page 143) as it works its way through a page or two of text, using the five roles. Ask the rest of the class to complete the Reciprocal Teaching Observation Sheet on page 157 while watching the model group.

2. Lead a discussion about reciprocal teaching roles. Ask the class to review the roles of the predictor, questioner, clarifier, summarizer, and discussion director while you record their responses on a piece of chart paper. Use the chart as a reminder of the tasks for each role.

3. Show students the five role sheets and review the instructions on each sheet.

4. Because the discussion director role is different for fiction and nonfiction, ask the model groups to demonstrate an example with each kind of text. For fiction, the discussion director leads the group after reading in discussing text-to-self, text-to-text, and text-to-world connections. For nonfiction, the discussion director leads the group before reading in creating a What We Know and What We Wonder Chart (page 164).

1. Before asking all students to work on their own in literature circles, try one of the following ideas:

   • Use jigsaw groups (Kagan, 1989). Break the class into five expert strategy groups—the predictors, questioners, clarifiers, summarizers, and discussion directors. Have the students meet in their expert groups to discuss only their role and the reading material. Give each expert group the appropriate role sheet (see pages 151–154, and 155 or 156). You might meet briefly with each expert group to assist students in their strategy use as they prepare to meet in reciprocal teaching literature circles. Then, have students form literature circles that include one person for each of the five roles.

   • Meet with one literature circle at a time, and either assign roles or let the group members choose roles. Have the rest of the class stay at their desks, reading quietly. As the literature circle works its way through the reciprocal teaching strategy roles, you may guide the students or make suggestions. After working with one group, send its members back to their seats and call another group to work with you in a literature circle.

   • Have students in literature circles rotate roles until each student has had a chance to play each role. See the Steps to Rotating Roles in Reciprocal Teaching Literature Circles on page 165.

   • Have students meet in literature circles with role sheets, and have the discussion director in each group complete the Literature Discussion Sheet for Reciprocal Teaching (page 141) to record the group member's responses. See Figure 26 for a student sample.

2. After students have worked in expert groups or have met with you in literature circles, have them work on their own in literature circles. You may, however, circulate around the room to assist groups when necessary.

Assessment Tips

   • The discussion directors can run a brief reflection at the end of the literature circle session. The group members should reflect on their strategy use and social skills and offer one another compliments and suggestions for improvement.

- Call on the discussion directors to report to the whole class how their group did that day in strategy use and social skills. Their classmates can offer suggestions for groups who are having trouble with reciprocal teaching strategies or social skills such as taking turns, listening to one another, and commenting politely.

Figure 26
Cecily's Record of Her Literature Circle's Work
on the Literature Discussion Reciprocal Teaching Sheet

Cecily

Group Members: Hank, Robbie, Lindsay

Literature Discussion
Reciprocal Teaching Sheet

Predict	**Question**
Fiction	Here are questions I can ask my group
I predict that	(who, what, when, where, why , how, what
Keith's Mom's will find Ralph in the waste basket and th	if..)
because there is a picture of Keith's Mom really disliked and she hates mice.	1. What was Ralph eating? and what did he save for dessert?
Nonfiction	2. What was he hoping would fall on him?
I think I will learn_____	
	3. What two things went over the top of the waste basket
_because_____	

Summarize	**Clarify**
Here is a one or two sentence summary.	1. Kleenex is a difficult word because (for a 1st grader)
Ralph is stuck in the waste basket and can't get out. Ralph is afraid when the trash is thrown out the boys will be looking and looking for his motorcyle. then Ralph falls asleep	of the X might be difficult to say.
	So I tried (check strategies you used)
	✓ checked parts of the word I know.
	_sounded the word out.
	_thought of a word that looks like this.
	_read on to find clues
	_reread to find clues
	_tried another word.
	2._____is a confusing idea because_____
	So I tried (check the strategies you used)
	__I reread
	__I read on.
	__I thought about what I know.
	__I talked to a friend..

We are reading The mouse and the Motorcyle by Beverly Cleary

161

- Vary the written responses of groups. Collect a group's Literature Discussion Sheet for Reciprocal Teaching that one member has recorded for the other students. On other occasions, you can ask each group member to fill out one of the sheets. Use these written records as a way to find out which students need help with certain strategies.

- If your students are having trouble with summaries, ask each group to submit a group summary and share it with the class. Have the class vote on the best summary (Hacker & Tenent, 2002).

- Use the rubric in Appendix A on page 195 to guide your assessment, then teach the minilessons on pages 179–182 to groups of students who need reinforcement in particular strategies.

- Refer to the suggestions of Figure 4 (page 21) when your students are struggling.

- Encourage your students to assess themselves on the strategies and their participation in the literature circle using the Self-Assessment Form for Reciprocal Teaching Literature Circles (page 142).

Classroom Story

Fourth-Grade Intervention Students Become Reciprocal Teaching Experts

For four months, I have worked with six struggling fourth-grade readers, using reciprocal teaching strategies with them during guided reading lessons. I meet with the group one day a week, and the teachers' aide meets with them on another. Over the past months, we have told the students that the reason we are meeting with them is because they are going to be our "experts" in reciprocal teaching strategies and will eventually teach the strategies to the rest of the class during literature circles. We have found that this special purpose has boosted the students' attitudes, and they have looked forward to our intervention sessions. They often have asked, "When are we going to teach the rest of the class?" Finally, the day has arrived.

I gather the entire fourth-grade class and tell them that they will have the opportunity to focus on four important strategies to help them to become even stronger readers. I also inform them that I have called on six of their classmates to be our resident experts in the strategies. To get started, I ask the class to talk about some strategies that good readers use as they read. We have worked as a class on a more comprehensive list of reading strategies, so the students are prepared to discuss many good reader strategies. They respond that "Good readers predict or think about what will happen next," "We make connections to our selves," "Questions are important," "Good readers check to see if things make sense," and "Good readers make connections to other books."

Next, I give each student a Be the Teacher Bookmark, and I tell them that when we focus on these Fabulous Four strategies their reading comprehension can improve. I ask the class to tell me what they already know about the four strategies listed on the bookmarks. As I lead the ensuing discussion, the experts from the intervention group eagerly raise their hands and share their knowledge. They share the following information with their classmates:

"Predictions have to be made using clues from the book."

"Clarifying helps you to understand words or ideas that are hard. Then, you need a plan for fixing them."

"Summarizing is when you take only the important stuff and tell it in order."

"Questioning is so fun. As you read, you look for really good places to ask your friends questions. You need to know the answers."

Today, the class will apply these strategies to *Grandfather's Journey* (Say, 1993) during literature circles. To model briefly how the literature circles will flow, I ask the experts to sit in a circle on the floor at the front of the room. I place the rotating roles cards—which include guidelines for a discussion director, clarifier, summarizer, predictor, and questioner—on the floor in the center of their circle. I tell the class that although we are focusing on the Fabulous Four strategies, we need to include a few strategies such as connecting and tasks such as making a chart.

At this point, each student chooses a role card. Juana chooses the predictor card and begins by asking the group to look at the text's illustrations and make a prediction. Then, the discussion director, Eric, asks the group how they want to read the book today, and they decide to read chorally. After reading the first page aloud, they stop and the discussion director calls on the summarizer, questioner, and clarifier to take turns giving their responses. Then, the predictor shares a prediction for what may happen next. Finally, the discussion director tells the students to pass their cards to the person on their right. Each student receives a new card and role for reading the next page of the story.

After the modeling session with the expert group, the class discusses what the expert group did well. Their comments include "They took turns" and "They summarized well." Then, I break up the group and assign one expert to each group of five other students so the experts can assist the other group members as they work their way through reciprocal teaching strategies. As I listen in on the groups, I am thrilled to see the struggling students taking the lead in the discussions. They model the strategies for their groups and assist other students in using the four strategies. As students pass the cards and rotate roles, I can hear the expert students saying,

"When you predict you need to use clues from the book."

"Can you find a word to clarify? Now tell how you will fix it."

"Can you make that summary shorter? You don't want it the same size as the page."

Reflection and Next Steps   Over the next few weeks, we will use reciprocal teaching literature circles with novels and the class's social studies text. Throughout the school year, we will continue to alternate between reciprocal teaching literature circles and traditional literature circles. Our goal is that the students will improve in their reading levels and their use of the four reciprocal teaching strategies.

What We Know and What We Wonder Chart

Names of group members: _____

Title and author of text: _____

What We Know
(What do you know about the topic? Each group member writes and shares an *I Know* strip and glues it below.)

What We Wonder
(What do we wonder about? After previewing the text and illustrations, each group member writes and shares an *I Wonder* strip and glues it below.)

Steps to Rotating Roles in Reciprocal Teaching Literature Circles

Roles: predictor, summarizer, clarifier, questioner, and discussion director

1. Each participant takes a role sheet.

2. The predictor begins by giving a prediction.

3. The discussion director selects the mode of reading for the page.

    • silent reading

    • reading aloud

    • reading with a partner

    • reading chorally

    • reading by paragraph or page

    After reading, the discussion director calls on or takes volunteers from the other roles—summarizer, questioner, and clarifier—in any order.

4. After a set number of pages, the discussion director calls "pass," and the literature circle participants pass their role sheets to the right.

5. The process begins again.

Adapted from a model by fourth-grade teachers Lynne Hyssop and Susan Preble at Hester School, San Jose, California.

Reciprocal Teaching at Work: Strategies for Improving Reading Comprehension by Lori D. Oczkus © 2003. Newark, DE: International Reading Association. May be copied for classroom use.

Lesson 3: Using What I Know and What I Wonder Strips

Predict

Question

Clarify

Summarize

Background and Description

In addition to predicting prior to reading, students also need opportunities in reciprocal teaching literature circles to activate their background knowledge and record what they want to know about a topic. This lesson completes reciprocal teaching literature circles with the additional strategies that good readers use before reading (Hoyt, 1999; Ogle, 1986).

Teachers at all grade levels can easily implement What I Know and What I Wonder strips with any nonfiction reading material, including articles, leveled books, and textbook chapters. For example, Mr. Herman's sixth-grade students worked independently at their desks prior to meeting with their literature circles to discuss a social studies chapter about ancient Greece. Each student wrote on two strips of paper. The first strip was for recording one fact that he or she knew about ancient Greece. After previewing the chapter's headings, illustrations, and maps, the students each wrote on the second strip something that they wondered about the topic. Later, during the literature circle session, the students shared their strips and posted them on a chart.

The What I Know and What I Wonder strips give you the opportunity to teach the whole class the additional background information and vocabulary necessary for understanding the reading material before a literature circle session. I use this lesson as a transitional, teacher-led step that prepares students for working with nonfiction materials in their reciprocal teaching literature circles. This lesson

- requires the activation of students' prior knowledge about a topic and
- encourages students to wonder about what the text will contain prior to reading it.

Tell your students how their prior knowledge helps them to understand what they read. Then, introduce your students to the background knowledge necessary for understanding the chosen text's topic. Teach your students how to wonder about a topic prior to reading, and show them how wondering helps to develop their reading comprehension.

Materials

- Two colored construction paper strips per student
- A piece of chart or construction paper for each literature circle
- A copy of the reading material for each student
- Tape or glue

Teacher Modeling

1. Tell your students that good readers think about what they know before they read, and then model that strategy. Preview the text's cover and title (or the first page if you have chosen a chapter). On a What I Know strip, write one fact that you know about the text's topic.

2. Next, tell your students that good readers wonder about the topic of a text that they are going to read. Show your students how to preview the illustrations and other graphics in the text that you have chosen.

   As you view the various items, say aloud what you are wondering. Write a What I Wonder statement on the second paper strip, using the opening phrase, "I wonder...."

Student Participation

1. Invite your students to work in cooperative table groups or pairs to come up with one What I Know strip and one What I Wonder strip about the chosen text. Have the groups share their strips and give a rationale for their statements.

2. Have your students individually preview the chapter or book again and come up with two more What I Know and What I Wonder strips with their names on them.

3. Have literature circles meet, and instruct their discussion directors to lead a sharing of the group members' What I Know and What I Wonder strips. Have each group tape or glue its strips onto the piece of chart or construction paper that you have provided (see Figure 27 for an example).

Figure 27
A Student Sample of the What We Know and What We Wonder Chart

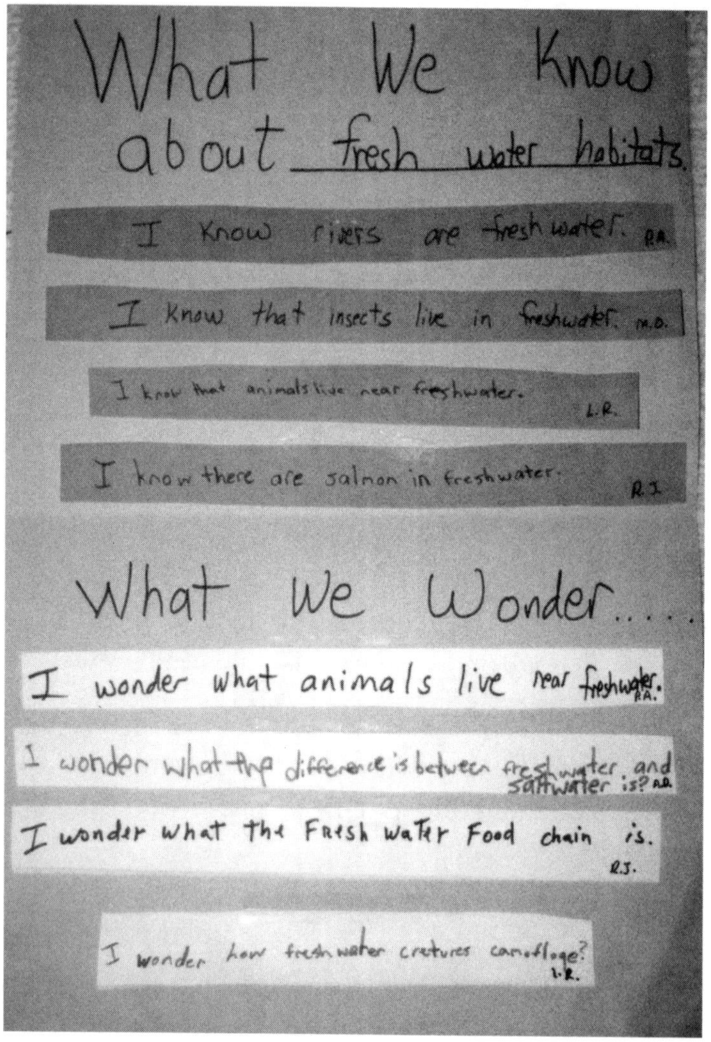

What We Know about fresh water habitats.

I Know rivers are fresh water. R.A.

I know that insects live in freshwater. M.O.

I know that animals live near freshwater. L.R.

I know there are salmon in freshwater. R.J.

What We Wonder.....

I wonder what animals live near freshwater. R.A.

I wonder what the difference is between freshwater and saltwater is? A.A.

I wonder what the Fresh Water Food chain is. R.J.

I wonder how freshwater creatures camouflage? L.R.

Assessment Tips

- Have each literature circle discuss how thinking about prior knowledge and questions before reading helps them learn to understand what they read.

- Collect your students' What I Know and What I Wonder strips. Ask yourself, Are my students activating appropriate background knowledge on the topic? Are they wondering about the text by using clues from the illustrations or the text prior to reading?

- Identify students who are having difficulty with the What I Know and/or What I Wonder Strips. Some students may need background information for a particular topic or may have difficulty studying illustrations and other text clues. Support these students in a small-group setting in which you model with both fiction and nonfiction texts how to wonder about a topic before reading.

- When your students need extra reinforcement in predicting with nonfiction texts, use the minilesson I Predict That I Will Learn... (page 179).

Lesson 4: Practicing Reciprocal Teaching Strategies With the Reciprocal Teaching Spinner

Predict

Question

Clarify

Summarize

Reciprocal Teaching Strategies in This Lesson

Background and Description

The fifth graders in Mrs. Nichols's class huddled around their Reciprocal Teaching Spinners in their literature circles. When the spinner in one group landed on *Question*, Jason enthusiastically blurted out, "Yeah! I finally got a question!" His question, based on the text that the group had read, was, "How many insects does a bat eat in one night?" Then, the rest of the group members watched intently as Nora took her turn with the spinner. "I hope I get *Clarify* because I have a great word to clarify this time," she explained. Nora landed on *Question*, too, and sighed, but she grinned as she asked, "What are some of the insects that bats eat?" The other students raised their hands to answer, and the spinning and discussing continued until all the group members had taken a turn.

The reciprocal teaching spinner is a useful, game-like tool to use with your students during reciprocal teaching in literature circles. The spinner strengthens reading comprehension skills by giving students the opportunity to use each reciprocal teaching strategy on multiple levels. However, similar to most of the activities and lessons in this chapter, the activity's success relies heavily on your students' proficiency and experience with reciprocal teaching strategies because they must be ready at any moment to model any of the four strategies.

You can make your own spinner and add other reading comprehension strategies such as making connections or include reaction prompts such as "My favorite part is..." or "I like the way that the author...."

Materials

- A Reciprocal Teaching Spinner (see form on page 172) made with tagboard for each literature circle
- A spinner (for each literature circle) made from a pencil and paper clip:
  1. Unbend the outer loop of a paperclip until it is straight.
  2. Place the paperclip onto the Reciprocal Teaching Spinner with the paperclip's remaining curved end directly over the spinner's center.
  3. Hold the paperclip in place by putting the point of a pencil into the clip's curved end.
  4. Spin the paperclip by quickly pushing the straightened section of it clockwise or counterclockwise.
- A copy of the reading material for each student in each group

Teacher Modeling

1. Ask your students to review all four reciprocal teaching strategies in table groups or in pairs. Using the Be the Teacher Bookmark (page 53), students take turns defining the strategies.

2. Read a page of text aloud to your students while they follow along. Then, spin the Reciprocal Teaching Spinner several times and model each reciprocal teaching strategy in regard to the text. When modeling predicting, demonstrate how to predict what may come next in the reading.

Student Participation

1. Select a group of students to model how to use the Reciprocal Teaching Spinner with a text that they have read. Discuss possible solutions when two students spin and land on the same strategy: Have the class decide if they should create a new prediction, summary, question, or clarification or perhaps add to the one that the other student previously generated.

2. Ask the class to discuss the model group's Reciprocal Teaching Spinner discussion. Elicit their compliments and suggestions, and discuss how the students can create another response when someone already has landed on the same strategy. The following list offers some examples:

- Predict: Come up with another possible prediction, or add a detail to the prediction that another student has made.

- Question: Ask another question using a different question word.

- Clarify: Choose another word or idea to clarify.

- Summarize: Repeat or improve the summary that another student has given.

Assessment Tips

- Ask your students to reflect on the reciprocal teaching strategy use in their literature circles. Which strategy did they hope they would land on with the spinner? Why? Observe the groups to see what students do when two of them in a row land on the same strategy. Does the second student copy the previous student's response or generate a new response?

- Teach the minilessons on pages 179–182 to either the entire class or small groups to reinforce the reciprocal teaching strategies. Evaluate your students' strategy use with the rubric in Appendix A on page 195.

Reciprocal Teaching Spinner

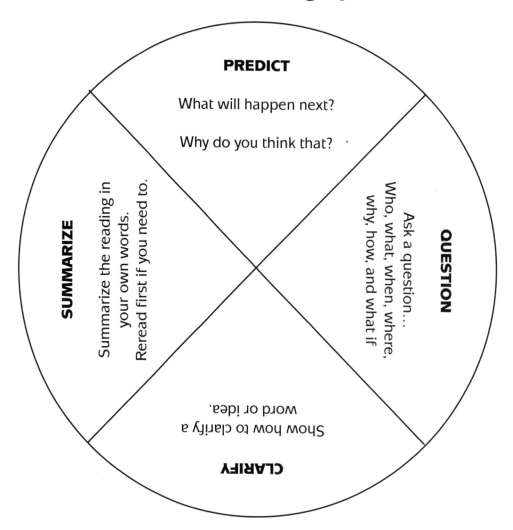

PREDICT

What will happen next?

Why do you think that?

QUESTION

Ask a question...
Who, what, when, where,
why, how, and what if

CLARIFY

Show how to clarify a
word or idea.

SUMMARIZE

Summarize the reading in
your own words.
Reread first if you need to.

When you land on a strategy that someone else already landed on, you can...

PREDICT
- Give a new prediction.
- Or, add a detail to the last one.

CLARIFY
- Choose another word or idea to clarify.
- Or, give more ways to clarify the same word or idea.

QUESTION
- Ask another question that begins with a different question word.

SUMMARIZE
- Give a new summary.
- Or, add to the previous summary.

Lesson 5: Organizing Cross-Age Buddy Sessions With Reciprocal Teaching

Predict

Question

Clarify

Summarize

Reciprocal Teaching Strategies in This Lesson

Background and Description

Mr. Metzer's fifth graders and Miss Clark's first graders met in cross-age pairs to focus on summarizing, and all the pairs had copies of *Ira Sleeps Over* (Waber, 1987). Mr. Metzer wanted his fifth graders to feel very confident in their summaries, so the class has practiced summarizing prior to the lesson with their little buddies. The little buddies also have been practicing how to summarize with their grade-level anthology and are ready to share brief summaries of the most recently read selection with their big buddies.

The little buddies streamed into the fifth-grade classroom and awaited the usual cross-age buddy read-aloud. This time, each big buddy asked the little buddy if he or she knows how to summarize. The little buddies eagerly shared the summaries that they created for the selection from the anthology. Then, the big buddies began reading *Ira Sleeps Over*, and after they read a page the cross-age pairs stopped to take turns summarizing what had happened on the page. After reading the whole book, the cross-age pairs constructed brief, written summaries of it and created drawings to accompany their summaries.

Next, each cross-age pair joined with another pair in a cross-age literature circle. The pairs took turns in the circles to share their summaries and drawings for *Ira Sleeps Over*. Then, they took turns asking questions and clarifying words and confusing parts of the book. When both buddy classes are engaged in instruction with reciprocal teaching strategies, the cross-age buddy sessions become a perfect opportunity to reinforce the strategies.

Similar to the above example, this lesson has suggestions for strengthening your students' use of reciprocal teaching strategies during cross-age buddy sessions. You also may choose to use the chapter minilessons (pages 179–182) with cross-age buddies to focus on particular strategies.

This lesson requires detailed descriptions of the steps for using each strategy. Also, continue discussing read-aloud techniques for big buddies. Explain that to keep the little buddies' attention, big buddies may wish to try engaging in a picture preview before reading, predicting periodically while reading, and allowing the buddies to ask questions during and after reading.

Materials

- A Be the Teacher Bookmark (page 53) for each student
- Focused Strategy Lessons to Use With Your Little Buddy (see form on page 177)
- Copies of texts with which to model reciprocal teaching strategies (one per cross-age pair)
- Copies of texts for your students to read to and with their buddies (one per cross-age pair)

Teacher Modeling

1. Before meeting as cross-age buddies, the students from both grade levels should work on reciprocal teaching strategies in their own classes with grade-appropriate lessons. Both teachers will want to familiarize their classes with the Be the Teacher Bookmark (page 53).

2. The big buddies' teacher should ask his or her students how their little buddies are doing with reciprocal teaching strategies and discuss the little buddies' progress. Identify which strategies the little buddies need to practice.

3. Ask the big buddies' class to vote on a focus strategy for the day that is based on what they think their little buddies all need to practice. Remind the big buddies that they will ask their little buddies to try all four reciprocal teaching strategies, but that they will spend more time modeling the focus strategy for their little buddies.

   As an option, choose a piece of literature to have the entire class of big buddies read as practice for the cross-age buddy session. If you do not have multiple copies of picture books available, then you might borrow the little buddies' reading series anthology for the big buddies to read aloud. Or, have the big buddies work with the focus strategy in any book that they select.

4. Invite a student volunteer from the class of big buddies to role-play as a little buddy. Using a picture book, demonstrate how to model a prediction, question, point or word to clarify, or summary for the little buddy. Then, invite a big buddy to do the same for each strategy. Model how to compliment the efforts of and support a struggling little buddy.

5. Model the focus strategy of the day. Show the big buddies how they can focus on the strategy of the day by having their little buddies stop either to draw or write about that strategy.

Student Participation

1. After observing the model lesson that uses the focus strategy, the big buddies should list the steps of that strategy on a class chart on chart paper or a whiteboard to help their little buddies.

2. Instruct the big buddies to try the focus strategy first with a peer partner. They should elicit a written response or drawing from their partner to save for the class debriefing.

3. Have the big buddies try the focus strategy lesson with their little buddies, and ask them to bring the little buddies' written responses or drawings back to your classroom for the debriefing.

4. Instruct each cross-age pair to join another cross-age pair to form a literature circle where they can share responses to the focus strategy of the day and take turns with other reciprocal teaching strategies.

5. Ask the big buddies to report to their class on their little buddies' progress with the focus strategy. Encourage the big buddies to give specific examples of how their little buddies used the focus strategy and share the written responses and drawings. Plan a follow-up lesson together for the next cross-age buddy session.

6. Ask the big buddies to be prepared to give examples of how they used the focus strategy in their own reading. They may want to share their reflections with their peers and their little buddies in the next cross-age buddy session.

Assessment Tips

This lesson requires the big buddies to assess how their little buddies are doing with the four reciprocal teaching strategies. The goal is for the big buddies to become even more reflective in their own strategy use.

- Observe the big and little buddies during a minilesson as they work with their peers. Collect their writings and drawings and evaluate them to see who needs help.

- Observe all the students during cross-age buddy interactions. Watch for good examples to point out in debriefings and for students who are having trouble modeling or coaching the focus strategy.

- Encourage the big buddies to use the Assessment Tool to Assess How Your Little Buddy Is Doing (see form on page 178). Once the big buddy has determined which reciprocal teaching strategy needs reinforcement, he or she can choose a lesson from Focused Strategy Lessons to Use With Your Little Buddy (page 177).

- Have the big buddies share the writings and drawings from their cross-age buddy sessions. Ask them to plan another lesson that will help correct any problems that their little buddies are having with their reciprocal teaching focus strategy use.

- Use the minilessons from this chapter (pages 179–182) to reinforce reciprocal teaching strategies. Also, refer to Figure 4 (page 21) when you need extra suggestions for helping your students with each strategy.

Focused Strategy Lessons
to Use With Your Little Buddy

When your buddy needs extra work on predicting

- Show your buddy how to look at the cover and make predictions based on visual clues. Say, "I predict…because…," and then let your buddy try doing the same.
- Model how to look at the illustrations and tell what the book will be about.
- While reading, stop and show your buddy how to use clues from the words and pictures to predict what will happen next. Say, "I see _____ in the book, so I think _____ will happen next because _____."
  Let your buddy try to do the same.
- Draw or write your predictions with your buddy.

When your buddy needs extra work on questioning

- Choose a page from the book and read it for your buddy. Demonstrate how to make up a question and answer based on what you just read. Show your buddy how to create questions that start with *who*, *what*, *when*, *where*, *why*, *how*, and *what if*.
- Ask your buddy to try making up a question about a part of the book.
- Draw or write about your questions with your buddy.

When your buddy needs extra work on clarifying

- Choose a long or difficult word from the reading, and show your buddy how to figure it out. Give at least two ways to figure out the word (use the Clarifying Words Bookmark on page 95).
  Try looking for word parts and chunks that you know, sounding out the word, and rereading or reading on to see if it makes sense.
- Let your buddy try to clarify with another word.
- Choose a confusing idea or part from the reading and demonstrate how you figured it out. Choose from
  - rereading,
  - reading on for clues,
  - using what you know,
  - letting your buddy try with another part, and
  - drawing or writing about clarifying either a word or confusing part of the reading.

When your buddy needs extra work on summarizing

- Choose one page from the reading, and reread it aloud. Tell the buddy that you are going to summarize and tell only the important points. Summarize the page, then let your buddy try to summarize the next page.
- Next, show your buddy how to summarize an entire book. For fiction, say
  "This story takes place _____."
  "The main characters are _____."
  "A problem is _____."
  "A key event is _____."
  "Finally, the problem is solved when _____."
  For nonfiction, say
  "This book is about _____."
  "The most important points are _____."
- Let your buddy try summarizing a book.
- Draw or write a summary with your buddy.

Assessment Tool to Assess
How Your Little Buddy Is Doing

Predicting

The buddy is predicting well if he or she
- looks at the cover and illustrations for clues to make predictions, and
- gives predictions that make sense.

The buddy is having trouble predicting if he or she
- does not look at the cover or illustrations for clues to make predictions, or
- makes predictions that do not make sense.

Questioning

The buddy is asking questions well if he or she
- can ask a question,
- knows what a question is, and
- asks questions that make sense and have answers in the text.

The buddy is having trouble asking questions if he or she
- cannot make up a question,
- does not know what a question is and gives a statement instead, or
- makes up questions that do not have answers in the text.

Clarifying

The buddy can clarify well if he or she
- knows more than one way to figure out a word, including looking for parts that he or she knows, blending sounds together, rereading, and reading on for clues;
- knows how to figure out a difficult idea or part; and
- rereads.

The buddy is having trouble clarifying if he or she
- cannot use strategies to figure out words,
- does not know when he or she is stuck, or
- does not reread.

Summarizing

The buddy can summarize well if he or she
- can retell the reading in his or her own words,
- leaves out details that do not matter, and
- tells only the most important ideas.

The buddy is having trouble summarizing if he or she
- cannot remember the reading,
- tells details that do not matter,
- gets mixed up and summarizes out of order, or
- leaves out important parts.

Minilesson: I Predict That I Will Learn...

Description and Comprehension Strategies

Prior to meeting with the literature circle, students will preview a nonfiction text, and, based on text and illustration clues, they will predict what they think they will learn from the reading. Comprehension strategies include using text clues to predict.

Materials

one copy per student of a nonfiction book or article (each group may use a different text), self-stick notes, and a chart

Teacher Modeling

1. Select a nonfiction book or article and model how to preview the cover and illustrations to predict what you think you will learn from the reading.

2. Write at least one sentence on a self-stick note that starts with "I predict that I will learn...because..." and model the clues that led you to believe that you would learn about your prediction.

Student Participation

1. Invite your students to work alone or in pairs before joining their literature circles to write at least one "I predict I will learn...because..." statement. Ask some students to share their responses with the class. Assist students who are having trouble.

2. When the literature circles meet, have them share their ideas and post them on a group chart. Encourage your students to check their predictions after reading to see which ones were correct or which were changed during reading.

Assessment Tip

Are your students using the text clues to form logical predictions about the reading?

Minilesson: Question, Answer, and Pass

Description and Comprehension Strategies
Students write two kinds of questions about the text after reading. Literature circles participate in a question, answer, and pass game. Comprehension strategies include asking and answering different types of questions.

Materials
one copy per student of a fiction or nonfiction text that has a table of contents, and two colors of index cards (one of each color per student)

Teacher Modeling
1. Model how to ask a question that could be answered in the text. Write your question on a colored index card.

2. Model asking a question that requires using the text information, plus making an inference. Write your question on an index card of a different color.

3. Ask your students to tell you what they notice about both kinds of questions.

Student Participation
1. Before your students go to their literature circles, ask them each to write a text-based question and an inferential question on index cards of different colors.

2. Have your students share their questions with the class and discuss the types of questions.

3. Have your students meet in literature circles and each pass one of their index cards to the person on their right. The students should read the questions silently, answer them silently, and pass the index card to the right again.

   Have them continue until the cards are back to the owners. Then, the students should repeat the process with the cards of the other color.

4. Have your students discuss the questions: Which were some of their favorites and why?

Assessment Tip
Can your students ask both types of questions? Ask the literature circles to reflect on questioning. If any students are having difficulty, organize a small group to meet with and model this questioning lesson using material that they have already read.

Minilesson: Concentrate on Clarifying

Description and Comprehension Strategies

Students work independently to find two words from the text to clarify. They share their words with their literature circles and play a quick game of concentration with the words and the clarifying strategies. Comprehension strategies include clarifying words using a variety of techniques.

Materials

one copy of the text and two index cards per student

Teacher Modeling

1. Choose one word from a text that the class has read and model clarifying with that word. Write the word and the surrounding sentence on an index card. On another card, write two strategies for deciphering the word.

2. Ask your students to discuss what they noticed about what you just modeled. What are the steps to clarifying a word?

Student Participation

1. Before meeting with their literature circles, your students should choose two words from their reading to clarify. Instruct them to write each word and the surrounding sentence on one index card and their clarifying strategies for the word on another card.

2. Have your students share their index cards with their literature circles. Instruct them to lay all the cards face down. One group member should mix them up and arrange them in rows. The group members should take turns turning over two cards at a time. When they have a word and the corresponding clarifying strategy card, they can keep the match. The player with the most matched cards wins.

Assessment Tips

- Ask your students to reflect on the clarifying strategies in their literature circles. How does clarifying help them to read?
- Provide modeling for students who are having difficulty clarifying. Make sets of sample clarifying cards for students to match. Guide the struggling students in a small group by modeling how to create cards for the concentration game.

Minilesson: A "Clear" Summary

Description and Comprehension Strategies

Each literature circle writes a summary on an overhead transparency to share with the class. Students may write the summaries for fiction or nonfiction texts and discuss summarizing for either text type. Comprehension strategies include writing a concise, clear summary and choosing main points to include in the summary.

Materials

a copy of the text for each student, one overhead transparency per literature circle, transparency pens for each group, and an overhead projector

Teacher Modeling

1. Choose a text that is familiar to the class. Model writing a summary on the overhead projector and decorate it with a few illustrations.

2. Ask the class to name the steps involved in writing a clear, concise summary.

Student Participation

1. Have your students work in literature circles to create summaries of the text that they have read. They should write the summary on an overhead transparency, sign their names, and decorate the summary with illustrations. Make sure that they include the text's title and author on the transparency.

2. Ask the literature circles to share their summaries with the entire class.

3. Ask your students to reflect on what makes a good summary for both fiction and nonfiction. How are they similar and different?

Assessment Tips

- Can your students work in a group to write an effective summary that includes important events in order?
- Ask your students to reflect on how summarizing helps them to comprehend what they read. Provide extra support for students who are struggling by working with a small group to create a clear summary.

Used with permission of Sandy Buscheck, Del Rey School, Orinda, California.

CHAPTER SUMMARY

- The cooperative nature of reciprocal teaching, along with the built-in scaffolded support, makes it a natural match for student-led literature circles.

- Reciprocal teaching literature circles and other literature circle models can be used in the same classroom. For example, some teachers use the reciprocal teaching model for nonfiction texts and another model for fiction texts.

- Students must be trained in three main areas before they embark on reciprocal teaching literature circles: the four reciprocal teaching strategies, small-group social skills, and literature circle procedures.

- Training for reciprocal teaching literature circles may involve working with reciprocal teaching strategies and role sheets during teacher-led guided reading groups.

- Modeling reciprocal teaching literature circles with a peer group in front of the class is a helpful technique for training students.

- Primary school students benefit from learning to read with reciprocal teaching strategies in reciprocal teaching literature circles.

- Other important comprehension strategies that are not included in the four reciprocal teaching strategies can be incorporated into literature circles by designating a discussion director. This role involves activating students' prior knowledge, making connections, wondering about the text prior to reading, working with graphic organizers, encouraging open responses, and monitoring social skills.

- Variations on using the four strategies in literature circles include rotating roles through the group and using a Reciprocal Teaching Spinner (page 172).

- Assessment routines for literature circles include teacher observations, modeling with groups, peer evaluation, filling in forms for individual accountability, and student self-evaluations.

Reflections for Group Study, Self-Study, or Staff Development

1 Describe how reciprocal teaching strategies can enhance comprehension during literature circles.

2 How can you prepare students for literature circles during guided reading sessions?

3 What are three areas in which students need training prior to working in reciprocal teaching literature circles?

4 How do primary school students benefit from reciprocal teaching literature circles?

5 Describe the benefits of using role sheets during reciprocal teaching literature circles.

6 What is the purpose of having one reciprocal teaching literature circle model for the class?

7 How will you assess individuals and groups on their use of reciprocal teaching strategies and proper social skills?

8 What are some variations and activities to use during reciprocal teaching literature circles?

CONCLUSION

When teachers tell me that their main concern is that their students are not thinking about or understanding what they read, I know I have a proven, research-based set of lessons that I can share with them. One third-grade teacher told me that she feels that "Reciprocal teaching takes the mystery out of teaching reading." In my opinion, her words are accurate because I believe that reciprocal teaching makes reading comprehension strategies more tangible for teachers and students. The reciprocal teaching strategies of predicting, questioning, clarifying, and summarizing have become the essential tools that I use to teach children to read. Of course, I need to add graphic organizers and the other important good-reader strategies (McLaughlin & Allen, 2002) for a truly comprehensive reading comprehension program, but the Fabulous Four reciprocal teaching strategies continue to make an enormous difference in my teaching effectiveness.

There are so many convincing reciprocal teaching success stories. For instance, consider the struggling fourth graders in Berkeley, California, whose reading levels jumped from a second-grade to a fourth-grade level in the first three months of using reciprocal teaching in an intervention group. Or, consider Ebony, a fifth-grade struggling reader who, in addition to participating in reciprocal teaching in her classroom, also used the strategies to work with her cross-age buddy, a first grader. Ebony's achievement accelerated one grade level, and a year later she had maintained the growth. Then, there are the struggling fourth graders who participated in small-group guided reading sessions for three months and then successfully introduced reciprocal teaching strategies to their entire class in literature circles.

After just a few weeks of reciprocal teaching instruction, most teachers begin to notice subtle differences in their students' behavior, achievement, and attitudes. Struggling readers raise their hands more often to contribute to discussions and appear more confident when reading. Proficient readers engage even more efficiently with grade-level and more challenging texts. As you use reciprocal teaching with your students, you surely will experience your own set of success stories.

Common Questions About Reciprocal Teaching

This section contains a series of questions and answers whose purpose is to review the content of the book and to provide information that you may need as you teach your students reciprocal teaching strategies.

1. What are the four reciprocal teaching strategies? Where did they originate?

The four strategies—predict, question, clarify, and summarize—were originally studied by Palincsar and Brown in the early 1980s. The researchers first used the strategies in a paragraph-by-paragraph scaffolded approach with struggling middle school students. Palincsar and Brown and others expanded the research into and use of the strategies and discovered that reciprocal teaching strategies were beneficial to students in a variety of grade levels and settings, including peer groups and interventions (Carter, 1997; Palincsar, Brown, & Campione, 1989; Palincsar & Klenk, 1991, 1992).

Other researchers and curriculum developers (Cooper et al., 1999; Lubliner, 2001) have created lessons for reciprocal teaching, but they have carefully maintained the integrity and intent of its original design.

2. What results might I expect if I use reciprocal teaching consistently with my students?

I am always amazed at how quickly I begin to see results with reciprocal teaching. The research verifies that reciprocal teaching can yield results in a relatively short amount of time: Palincsar and Brown (1984) found that students who scored around 30% on a comprehension assessment scored 70–80% after just 15–20 days of instruction using reciprocal teaching. After one year, the students maintained the growth (Palincsar & Klenk, 1991). In the schools where I work, which are diverse ethnically and in terms of urban, suburban, and rural settings, the students' reading levels rise one half to one full grade level in just 18–20 reciprocal teaching sessions (usually two to three per week).

Even though positive growth may be measured in such a short period of time, I recommend continuing the reciprocal teaching instruction for approximately 76 lessons, or most of the school year, because researchers report even more dramatic results or formal gains in reading level after an average of this many lessons (Cooper et al., 2000). In one of the inner-city schools where I work, struggling readers experienced rapid growth of one to two years in reading level after just three months. By the end of the school year, three months later, more students reached the target level and some students advanced an additional grade level in reading ability as measured by the district's assessment measures and the Developmental Reading Assessment (Beaver, 2001).

3. Should I use reciprocal teaching with my struggling readers?
Absolutely. I began by using reciprocal teaching with struggling readers, and it is the number one intervention strategy that I recommend for grades 3–8. Cooper and his teacher-researcher colleagues (2000) decided that they wanted to develop an intervention for struggling readers, and they incorporated reciprocal teaching with some other proven components, such as rereading, graphic organizers, and written responses to literature, to create a research-based intervention plan. Their research findings were positive enough to convince me to try reciprocal teaching as an intervention. Every time I consistently use their plan (Cooper et al., 1999), the students experience one half to one full year's growth after three months of lessons given at least twice a week and anywhere from one to two year's growth after six months. I especially love to witness the improved confidence that these readers almost immediately experience with reciprocal teaching.

4. What about the rest of my students? Do they really need reciprocal teaching?
All students can benefit from reciprocal teaching because it is a useful study strategy that students can use throughout their school careers, including college. I often tell students that once they learn the four strategies, they can rely on them for the rest of their lives. Reciprocal teaching strategies can serve as study tools even in college.

5. But don't I use these four strategies already? How is reciprocal teaching different from what I am already doing with these strategies?
Most likely, you already teach your students to predict, question, clarify, and summarize. Reading programs and school-district objectives often include these strategies. However, the difference with reciprocal teaching is that the strategies are delivered as a multiple-strategy package used in concert with one another rather than as separate strategies to master one at a time. The aim of reciprocal teaching is for good readers to cycle through the four strategies—not necessarily in order—to make sense of a text. The National Reading Panel (National Institute of Child Health and

Human Development, 2000) suggests using cooperative learning with multiple strategies and highly recommends reciprocal teaching as an effective teaching practice that improves reading comprehension.

6. I am so busy that I can barely teach what I have on my agenda now. How can I fit reciprocal teaching strategies into what I am doing already?

You do not have to overhaul your curriculum to fit reciprocal teaching strategies into your schedule. After introducing the four strategies to your students, you can incorporate the strategies easily into lessons using the district-adopted texts for reading, social studies, and science. Some teachers even ask students to use predicting, questioning, clarifying, and summarizing during math lessons. Reciprocal teaching can be incorporated easily into your school day.

7. What is your best piece of advice for using reciprocal teaching?

Be consistent. If you really want results with struggling readers, use the strategies at least twice a week in an intervention group, and with the rest of the class use reciprocal teaching two to three times per week in either whole-class, guided reading, or literature circle settings. Using the strategies once a week or just a few times per month may help students somewhat, but students need consistent exposure to the strategies to benefit greatly from them.

8. What foundations must be in place to achieve the maximum results with reciprocal teaching?

Whether using reciprocal teaching in whole-class sessions, guided reading groups, or literature circles, there are some foundations that make the instruction more effective. These essentials include scaffolding, thinking aloud, using cooperative learning, and facilitating metacognition. Scaffolding is the umbrella for the other three foundations, and it simply means good teaching through teacher modeling that usually consists of a think-aloud and student participation with feedback from the teacher or peers. A scaffolded lesson also allows time for metacognition or reflection on the use of the strategies and how they helped the reader understand the text. When these components are in place, reciprocal teaching lessons may yield better results than if the foundations are not addressed.

9. If reciprocal teaching is so effective, why can't I just teach reading with the four strategies—predict, question, clarify, and summarize?

Reciprocal teaching strategies do work, but they do not stand alone. Throughout this book, I have emphasized the need for a more complete set of reading strategies to teach reading comprehension effectively. The expanded list of key research-based comprehension strategies comprises previewing, activating prior knowledge, predicting, self-questioning, making connections, visualizing, knowing how words work, monitoring, summarizing, and evaluating (McLaughlin & Allen, 2002).

10. What is the best way to get started with reciprocal teaching?

No one best way to begin using reciprocal teaching in your classroom exists. Any of the following models will work, or you can even develop your own combination. The key is to regularly model and practice the strategies with your students.

Get started with reciprocal teaching using one of the following models:

- Whole Class—Literature Circles—Whole Class
  In some classrooms, you can introduce the strategies to the whole class by using the Be the Teacher Bookmark (page 53) or the Introducing the Reciprocal Teaching Team—The Fabulous Four lesson (page 39). Then, continue to model reciprocal teaching strategies, using below-grade-level materials at first and eventually progressing to grade-level reading materials. After the class is comfortable with the strategies, introduce them to literature circles by modeling literature circle procedures in front of the class with a peer group. Finally, return to a whole-class setting, and take time to reflect on the strategies in a discussion.

- Intervention Group—Whole Class—Literature Circles
  This plan is the most innovative teaching model that I have used so far. In some classrooms, the classroom teacher and I spend several months working with the struggling students in an intervention group. During those months, we tell the struggling students that they will need to become experts in the four reciprocal teaching strategies so they can introduce them to the rest of the class. After about three months, the intervention students assist their classroom teacher in modeling the four strategies for the class. Then, the class is divided into literature circles, and the reciprocal teaching experts

from the intervention group are dispersed among the groups to lead them. I have witnessed struggling readers beam as they teach their class reciprocal teaching strategies. Even after this stage, however, the intervention group continues to meet to ensure the struggling students' progress.

- Guided Reading Groups—Whole Class—Guided Reading Groups
  I have used this model in grades 1–3 when students may need more time and a small-group format to catch on to reciprocal teaching strategies. The classroom teacher and I meet with the students in their guided reading groups, where we model and teach guided reading lessons using reciprocal teaching strategies. After several months, we begin to use the strategies in a whole-class setting with shared reading material such as Big Books and the district-adopted reading anthology. We may keep Be the Teacher Bookmarks (page 53) available for each student to use throughout the day as we weave the four strategies into our lessons. Finally, we organize guided reading groups that continue to use reciprocal teaching strategies.

11. How can I use reciprocal teaching with literature circles?
Literature circles are natural places to use reciprocal teaching because the four strategies can become the roles of predictor, questioner, clarifier, and summarizer. I have found that including the fifth role of discussion director is helpful for discussing other reading comprehension strategies such as making connections, activating prior knowledge, and inferring. There are many effective ways to incorporate reciprocal teaching strategies into literature circles at every grade level and with any kind of text.

12. What if I already have in place procedures and roles for literature circles that differ from reciprocal teaching?
If you already have literature circles in place, that is great because your students have been trained in the basic social skills of group work. Now, all you need to do is decide how to model for them the process of using the four strategies as roles (see chapter 4, especially Lessons 1 and 2).

Some intermediate teachers who already have in place literature circles using other models (for example, see Daniels, 1994) may opt to designate nonfiction texts and textbooks for use with reciprocal teaching strategies and roles, while maintaining another model for fiction texts. Another suggestion is to use reciprocal teaching with the school district-adopted anthology and use other literature circle models with novels or core literature. Keep in mind that reciprocal teaching works well with fiction or nonfiction texts.

13. How can I use literature circles with students in grades 1 and 2?

Primary teachers often prefer the simplicity of using just four roles with reciprocal teaching, and they often use reciprocal teaching with literature circles because the circles reinforce comprehension as students are learning to read. However, it is helpful to meet with students in grades 1 and 2 in guided reading groups first before expecting them to perform the reciprocal teaching strategies effectively in literature circles.

14. How can I use reciprocal teaching with my guided reading groups?

Guided reading is a great setting for using reciprocal teaching strategies with your students. The small-group atmosphere encourages participation from all students and allows you to assess their progress easily. You can use any reading materials that you already have to conduct reciprocal teaching lessons with guided reading groups. In regard to how to organize the groups, I organize my groups flexibly, changing them depending on the needs or interests of the students.

Lead a guided reading group through reciprocal teaching strategies by taking turns with the students as they work their way through the strategies and the reading. First, discuss illustrations and headings and take turns making predictions. Then, instruct your students to read silently or with partners while you quietly coach individual students. After reading, take turns again asking questions about the text, summarizing, and discussing points or words that your students need to clarify. Throughout the lesson, I usually fill in a guided reading chart that fits the text and lesson (see the charts in Lesson 2 of chapter 3).

I have found that the guided reading setting offers an effective training ground for literature circles. After all the groups have worked with me to learn the four strategies and group procedures, I begin to introduce them to reciprocal teaching literature circles. After I start working with the students in literature circles, I do not discontinue the guided reading groups. I meet with the groups for reciprocal teaching lessons because students continue to benefit from the small-group format.

15. Are there any common problems that students experience with reciprocal teaching?

Some students may experience difficulty when first learning reciprocal teaching strategies. Their problems may include the following:

- Predicting: Students may not make logical predictions based on clues from the text or their experiences.

- Questioning: Students may generate only literal questions and may need more modeling in or guidance toward asking inferential or main idea questions.

- Clarifying: Students may initially clarify only difficult, new, or confusing words because students rarely recognize that they are having trouble with an idea in the text.

- Summarizing: Students may miss the main points of a given selection, or they may supply a summary that is too long, too short, or a word-by-word rendition from the text.

To avoid these common problems, I recommend teaching the minilessons at the end of each chapter that focus on a particular strategy that is causing your students difficulty. Also, daily teacher modeling and peer practice help students to catch on to the strategies.

16. With reciprocal teaching, how can I foster higher order reading skills such as making inferences and evaluating?

Inferring and other higher order reading skills are already embedded in the reciprocal teaching strategies. For example, when students predict, they engage in making a type of inference. Inferring involves drawing a conclusion by gathering clues or evidence from the text and one's own background knowledge. During questioning, encourage your students to ask inferential and evaluative questions. As your students summarize, ask them to think about the selection's theme or the author's message. When they clarify ideas in a text, your students may link points of confusion in the text with higher order questions that they have about the text's content or the author's intent. As you can see, there are many opportunities to include higher order reading skills during reciprocal teaching lessons.

Improve Your Students' Reading Comprehension With Reciprocal Teaching

Whether you read this book from cover to cover or simply skip around and try various lessons, I hope you are motivated to use reciprocal teaching with your students. If you are new to reciprocal teaching, this book contains a wealth of resources to get you started and keep you going. If you already teach with the Fabulous Four reciprocal teaching strategies, this book offers many effective and innovative ways to enhance your use of reciprocal teaching. It is my goal that you will try reciprocal teaching strategies with your students and witness for yourself the difference this proven set of reading strategies can make in the reading comprehension skills of all students.

I encourage feedback and questions, which can be sent to me at loczkus52@earthlink.net.

A Rubric for
RECIPROCAL TEACHING:
What to Look for When Observing Students

Predicting

When predicting with fiction, students

• preview the front and back covers, illustrations, and headings before reading;

• predict what is likely to happen next based on clues from the text or illustrations;

• use what they know (from text and prior knowledge);

• stop to predict during reading; and

• continue to make logical predictions based on clues from the text.

When predicting with nonfiction, students

• preview the front and back covers, illustrations, and headings before reading;

• predict what is likely to be learned based on clues from the text or illustrations;

• apply what they already know to help make a prediction;

• stop to predict during reading; and

• continue to make logical predictions based on clues from the text.

When using metacognition with either fiction or nonfiction, students tell how predicting helps them to understand the text.

The language of prediction that students use (Mowery, 1995) may include the following phrases:

• I think…because…

• I'll bet…because…

• I wonder if…because…

• I imagine…because…

• I suppose…because…

• I predict….because…

Questioning

When questioning with fiction, students

- ask questions based on the text (that is, the answers are in the text),

- ask questions that are based on the main idea or question of the story,

- ask some detail-oriented questions, and

- ask some inferential questions.

When questioning with nonfiction, students

- ask questions based on the text (that is, the answers are in the text);

- ask questions that are based on the main idea of the reading;

- ask some detail-oriented questions;

- ask questions based on nonfiction text features such as maps, captions, and diagrams; and

- ask some inferential questions.

When using metacognition for either fiction or nonfiction, students can tell how asking questions helps them to understand the text.

The language of questioning that students use may include the following words:

- who,

- what,

- when,

- where,

- why,

- how, and

- what if.

Clarifying

When clarifying with fiction, students

• express confusion with specific portions of text, such as ideas or events, that are difficult to understand and

• identify words that are difficult to pronounce or understand.

When clarifying with nonfiction, students

• point out confusing ideas related to the content of the reading;

• point out confusing portions of text such as sentences, paragraphs, and pages; and

• identify words that are difficult to pronounce or understand.

When using metacognition for either fiction or nonfiction, students

• give strategies for clarifying words,

• tell strategies for clarifying ideas, and

• tell how clarifying helps them to understand text.

The language of clarifying that students use may include the following phrases:

• I didn't understand the part about…, so I (see list below);

• This doesn't make sense, so I (see list below); and

• I can't figure out…, so I (see list below).

So I…

• reread, reread, reread;

• read on for clues;

• checked the parts of the word I knew;

• blended the sounds of the word;

• reread the sentence to see if it made sense; or

• tried another word.

Summarizing

When summarizing fiction, students

- retell the story in their own words and include the setting, characters, problem, key events, and resolution.

Or, they

- give only key points in a short one- or two-sentence summary,
- summarize in a logical order,
- reread to remember main ideas, and/or
- refer to illustrations to retell or summarize the text.

When summarizing nonfiction, students

- retell the key points or ideas,
- leave out unnecessary details,
- summarize in a logical order,
- reread to remember main ideas, and/or
- refer to illustrations, headings, and other text features to retell or summarize the text.

When using metacognition for either fiction or nonfiction, students tell how summarizing helps them to understand the text.

The language of summarizing that students use may include the following words or phrases:

- First,…
- Next,…
- Then,…
- Finally,…
- The most important ideas in this text are…
- The story takes place…
- The main characters are…
- A problem occurs when…
- A key event is when…
- This part is about…
- This book is about…

Reciprocal Teaching at Work: Strategies for Improving Reading Comprehension by Lori D. Oczkus © 2003. Newark, DE: International Reading Association. May be copied for classroom use.

Student
Self-Assessment for
RECIPROCAL
TEACHING

Using the Reciprocal Teaching Team When I Read

Please check off your answers.

How am I predicting?

Before reading

____ I preview the front and back cover.

____ I study the illustrations and headings.

____ I make predictions using clues from the text.

During reading

____ I stop and use clues from the reading to make more predictions or to change my predictions.

After reading

____ I check my predictions to see if they came about in the text.

Predicting helps me read because ____

_____

_____

_____

_____

How am I questioning?

Before reading

____ After previewing the cover, illustrations, and headings, I ask questions about the reading. What do I wonder or want to know?

During reading

____ As I read, I watch for answers to my questions.

____ As I read, I watch for places where a teacher could ask a question.

After reading

____ I check to see if I answered my questions.

____ I have questions that start with *who, when, where, what, why, how,* or *what if.*

Questioning helps me read because __

_____

How am I clarifying?

Before reading

____ I can tell what might look confusing about the reading.

____ I see some words when I am previewing the text that might be difficult or confusing.

During reading

____ I stop and think about words that are difficult.

____ I try chunking, sounding out, and rereading words.

____ I stop to clarify confusing ideas by rereading, reading on, or asking a friend.

After reading

____ I think about confusing or difficult words and ideas. I go back and figure them out by rereading or talking with a friend.

Clarifying helps me read because ____

_____

How am I summarizing?

Before reading

____ I think about how the text is organized.

During reading

____ I stop to think about what has happened so far in the reading.

After reading

____ I reread and review the illustrations to keep the reading fresh in my mind.

____ I choose only the main ideas to summarize.

____ I tell the main events in order.

Summarizing helps me read because

_____

_____

_____

_____

_____

_____

Informal Assessment Strategy Interviews

ssess your students' knowledge of the strategies and their metacognition in an informal, one-on-one interview. Ask the following questions, and have your students respond either verbally or in writing.

1. Which of the four reciprocal teaching strategies would you like to talk about first?
2. Define the strategy.
3. Explain how you use the strategy to help you understand what you read.

If a student has difficulty defining a particular strategy or telling how that strategy helps him or her read, assist the child in defining the strategy and its use. Then, make a note of the student's difficulty, and in future lessons group students who have difficulty with the same strategy and provide minilessons on that strategy from the various chapters in this book.

The following quotes resulted from individual strategy interviews:

"Each time in the beginning of a story of chapter, I like to predict what it is going to be about and after I read I like to see if I'm right. It's like estimation in math because with both you predict in the beginning and then see if you are right." —Belinda, grade 3

"Prediction is when you say what you think is going to happen in the book and you look at all the clues like the cover, pictures, and chapter headings." —Rachael, grade 4

"Predicting helps me so I could use my own imagination and think about whether the prediction happens or not." —Francisco, grade 4

"We use questioning to ask questions like a teacher." —Michelle, grade 5

"It depends on the level of the kid, how hard I make the question." —Stephani, grade 4

"You think of a question when you are reading the book, that you can ask someone who is also reading the book. You can ask an easy or hard question. When you are reading and you have a question about what you are reading, you can ask a friend." —Jacob, grade 3

"Clarify is when there is a hard word and you try to think of what it means. Also, clarify is when there is a part you don't understand and you look back in the parts that you already read. It is like a puzzle and you see if there is a piece missing." —Rachael, grade 4

"I like to clarify words and explain how you figure them out like sounding them out, looking for little words you know, and looking for syllables. Clarify helps me learn more words." —Belinda, grade 3

"Clarify is when you go back if you don't understand and look at the text again. If it's a sentence you don't really understand, you could reread it. If it's a word, you can look for a part you know, syllables, or sound it out." —Jacob, grade 3

"Clarify is when you look back at the sentence to gather clues about the word you don't know." —Tanya, grade 6

"Summarizing is a way to share in your own words what the story is about. It helps you by understanding it easier." —Carlin, grade 3

"In your own words, you tell what happened in the text."
—Francisco, grade 4

"If somebody hasn't read the book for awhile, you can summarize to tell them what's happening. If you need to catch up with a book on your own, you can read through parts of the book and start remembering what was happening in the story." —Jacob, grade 3

"After every chapter, I summarize to let people know what's going on so far. It helps you know what you're reading." —Belinda, grade 3

REFERENCES

Beaver, J. (2001). *Developmental reading assessment.* Upper Saddle River, NJ: Pearson Education.

Carter, C.J. (1997). Why reciprocal teaching? *Educational Leadership, 54*(6), 64–68.

Clay, M.M. (1985). *Early detection of reading difficulties* (3rd ed.). Portsmouth, NH: Heinemann.

Clay, M.M. (1993). *Reading Recovery: A guidebook for teachers in training.* Portsmouth, NH: Heinemann.

Cooper, J.D. (1993). *Literacy: Helping children construct meaning* (2nd ed.). Boston: Houghton Mifflin.

Cooper, J.D., Boschken, I., McWilliams, J., & Pistochini, L. (1999). *Soar to success: The intermediate intervention program.* Boston: Houghton Mifflin.

Cooper, J.D., Boschken, I., McWilliams, J., & Pistochini, L. (2000). A study of the effectiveness of an intervention program designed to accelerate reading for struggling readers in the upper grades. In T. Shanahan & F.V. Rodriguez-Brown (Eds.), *49th yearbook of the National Reading Conference* (pp. 477–486). Chicago: National Reading Conference.

Cunningham, P.M., & Cunningham, J.W. (1992). Making words: Enhancing the invented spelling-decoding connection. *The Reading Teacher, 46,* 106–115.

Daniels, H. (1994). *Literature circles: Voice and choice in the student-centered classroom.* York, ME: Stenhouse.

Donahue, P.L., Voekl, K.E., Campbell, J.R., & Mazzeo, J. (1999). *The NAEP 1998 reading report card for the nation and the states.* Washington, DC: National Center for Education Statistics.

Fielding, L., Anderson, R.C., & Pearson, P.D. (1990). *How discussion questions influence children's story understanding* (Tech. Rep. No. 490). Urbana, IL: University of Illinois, Center for the Study of Reading.

Flint, A.S. (1999). *Literature circles.* Westminster, CA: Teacher Created Materials.

Fountas, I.C., & Pinnell, G.S. (1996). *Guided reading: Good first teaching for all children.* Portsmouth, NH: Heinemann.

Hacker, D.J., & Tenent, A. (2002). Implementing reciprocal teaching in the classroom: Overcoming obstacles and making modifications. *Journal of Educational Psychology, 94*(4), 699–718.

Hammond, D. (1991). Prediction chart. In J.M. Macon, D. Bewell, & M. Vogt, *Responses to literature: Grades K–8* (pp. 11–12). Newark, DE: International Reading Association.

Hansen, J. (1981). The effects of inference training and practice on young children's reading comprehension. *Reading Research Quarterly, 16,* 391–417.

Hiebert, E., & Taylor, B. (Eds). (1994). *Getting reading right from the start: Effective early literacy interventions.* Boston: Allyn & Bacon.

Hill, B.C., Johnson, N.J., & Noe, K.S. (1995). *Literature circles and response.* Norwood, MA: Christopher-Gordon.

Hoyt, L. (1999). *Revisit, reflect, retell: Strategies for improving reading comprehension.* Portsmouth, NH: Heinemann.

Johnson, D.W., & Johnson, R.T. (1992). What to say to advocates for the gifted. *Educational Leadership, 50*(2), 44–47.

Kagan, S. (1989). *Cooperative learning resources for teachers.* San Juan Capistrano, CA: Resources for Teachers.

Keene, E.O., & Zimmermann, S. (1997). *Mosaic of thought: Teaching comprehension in a reader's workshop.* Portsmouth, NH: Heinemann.

Kohn, A. (1996). *Beyond discipline: From compliance to community.* Alexandria, VA: Association for Supervision and Curriculum Development.

Kulik, J.A., & Kulik, C.L. (1992). Meta-analytic findings on grouping programs. *Gifted Child Quarterly, 36*(2), 73–77.

Lipson, M.W. (1996). *Developing skills and strategies in an integrated literature-based reading program.* Boston: Houghton Mifflin.

Lubliner, S. (2001). *A practical guide to reciprocal teaching.* Bothell, WA: Wright Group.

McLaughlin, M., & Allen, M.B. (2002). *Guided comprehension: A teaching model for grades 3–8.* Newark, DE: International Reading Association.

Mowery, S. (1995). *Reading and writing comprehension strategies.* Harrisburg, PA: Instructional Support Team Publications.

National Institute of Child Health and Human Development. (2000). *Report of the National Reading Panel. Teaching children to read: An evidence-based assessment of the scientific research literature on reading and its implications for reading instruction* (NIH Publication No. 00-4769). Washington, DC: U.S. Government Printing Office.

National Reading Panel. (2000). *Put reading first: The research building blocks for teaching children to read.* Washington, DC: Author.

Ogle, D. (1986). K-W-L: A teaching model that develops active reading of expository text. *The Reading Teacher, 39,* 564–570.

Opitz, M.F. (1998). *Flexible grouping in reading: Practical ways to help all students become better readers.* New York: Scholastic.

Opitz, M.F., & Rasinski, T. (1998). *Good-bye round robin: 25 effective oral reading strategies.* Portsmouth, NH: Heinemann.

Palincsar, A.S., & Brown, A.L. (1984). Reciprocal teaching of comprehension-fostering and comprehension-monitoring activities. *Cognition and Instruction, 2,* 117–175.

Palincsar, A.S., & Brown, A.L. (1986). Interactive teaching to promote independent learning from text. *The Reading Teacher, 39,* 771–777.

Palincsar, A.S., Brown, A.L., & Campione, J. (1989). *Structured dialogues among communities of first-grade learners.* Paper presented at the annual meeting of the American Educational Research Association, San Francisco, California.

Palincsar, A.S., Brown, A.L., & Martin, S.M. (1987). Peer interaction in reading comprehension instruction. *Educational Psychologist, 22*(3/4), 231–253.

Palincsar, A.S., & Klenk, L. (1991). *Learning dialogues to promote text comprehension* (PHS Grant 059). Bethesda, MD: National Institute of Health and Human Development.

Palinscar, A.S., & Klenk, L. (1992). Fostering literacy learning in supportive contexts. *Journal of Learning Disabilities, 25*(4), 211–225.

Pearson, P.D., Roehler, L.R., Dole, J.A., & Duffy, G.G. (1992). Developing expertise in reading comprehension. In S.J. Samuels & A.E. Farstrup (Eds.), *What research has to say about reading instruction* (2nd ed., pp. 145–199). Newark, DE: International Reading Association.

INDEX

A

ABILITY GROUPS, 82, 83*f*

ADAMSON, S.C., 138

ALLEN, M.B., 2–3, 5, 14, 25–26, 41, 45, 49, 60, 91, 102, 122, 135, 144, 158, 185, 189

ALLINGTON, R.L., 88

ANDERSON, R.C., 15

ASSESSMENT IN RECIPROCAL TEACHING, 25, 195–199; in coaching in reciprocal teaching, 112; in cross-age buddy sessions, 176, 178; in guided reading, 87–89; in guided reading plan for fiction and nonfiction, 94, 100; interviews on, informal, 204–206; in introducing literature circles, 147; in introducing reciprocal teaching strategies, 44–45; in literature circles, 139–140; self-assessment form for, 142, 201–202; in using Be the Teacher bookmark, 52; in using Clarifying bookmarks, 123; in using comprehension charts, 104–106; in using cooperative table groups, 56; in using different types of reading materials, 60–64, 63*f*; in using movie or television clips and freeze frames, 120; in using reciprocal teaching spinner, 171; in using role sheets, 160–162; in using What I Know and What I Wonder strips, 168–169; in whole-class sessions, 38–39

B

BEAVER, J., 187

BECK, I., 5

BE THE TEACHER bookmark, 53; using, 49–52, 51*f*

BE THE TEACHER strategies, 14

BIG BOOKS: assessment with, 63*f*; using reciprocal teaching with, 61*f*

BLACHOWICZ, C., 5

BLOCK, C.C., 5

BOOK, C., 5

BOOKMARKS: Be the Teacher, 49–52, 53; Clarifying, 95, 121–123

BOOK SELECTION: for literature circles, 135

BOREDOM: approaches to, 20*f*

BOSCHKEN, I., 2–4, 6–7, 25–26, 59, 77, 81–82, 87, 98, 186–187

BROWN, A.L., 1–3, 6, 15, 26, 41, 134, 186

BUDDY SESSIONS: cross-age, 173–178

BUSCHECK, S., 182

C

CALDWELL, J., 38

CAMPBELL, J.R., 1

CAMPIONE, J., 6, 186

CARTER, C.J., 3, 6, 186

CHAPTER BOOKS: assessment with, 63*f*; using reciprocal teaching with, 62*f*

CHIOLA-NAKAI, D., 138

CLARA THE CAREFUL CLARIFIER, 40

CLARIFIER ROLE, 133; role sheet, 153

CLARIFYING, 1, 16–18; assessment of, 198; bookmarks, 95, 121–123; group poster, 126; minilesson on, 69–70, 181; problems with, overcoming, 21*f*

CLASSROOM: noisy, approach to, 20*f*

CLASSROOM STORIES: on coaching in reciprocal teaching, 113–115; on introducing literature circles, 147–150; on introducing reciprocal teaching strategies, 45–47; on using comprehension charts, 106–108; on using different types of reading materials, 64–66; on using role sheets, 162–163

CLAY, M.M., 76, 114